Steps of Understanding

Key events in Jesus' life

Gerald Bray

Christian Focus

© Gerald Bray

ISBN 185792 420 7

Published in 1998
by Christian Focus Publications
Geanies House, Fearn, Ross-shire, IV20 1TW, Great Britain

Cover design by Donna Macleod

Contents

1. The Pre-existence of Christ 5

2. The Annunciation 16

3. The Incarnation 26

4. The Baptism of Jesus 36

5. The Temptations of Jesus 47

6. The Transfiguration 59

7. The Crucifixion 69

8. The Resurrection 81

9. The Ascension 91

10. The Heavenly Session of Christ 102

11. The Second Coming of Christ 114

Preface

This collection of studies in the life of Jesus began life many years ago as a series of articles on different aspects of Christian doctrine, which appeared in the journal *Evangel* in the years 1984-6. They were well received at the time, but it was not until I was approached by Malcolm Maclean of Christian Focus Publications that I thought seriously of putting them in a more permanent form. Together we chose six of the original twelve articles, and decided to group them around the life of Jesus. This entailed adding other chapters to fill in the gaps left by the original series, and these have been written freshly for this book. Revising the earlier chapters was a more difficult task than I had imagined it would be, but I think that the result is a more coherent presentation than would otherwise have been the case.

I am very grateful to Mr Maclean and his staff at Christian Focus for the interest that they have shown in publishing this material, and I pray that it may be of help to the wider Christian public. We live in dangerous times, when it is easy to follow the way of the world and to forget our Lord. Perhaps it has always been so, but it is my prayer that those who read this book may be turned back again to Him who is the source of our life, and whom we are called to love and serve with all our heart, all our soul, all our mind and all our strength.

Gerald Bray

1

The Pre-existence of Christ

'In the beginning was the Word, and the Word was with God, and the Word was God.' The opening line of John's Gospel is one of the most famous, and at the same time, one of the most difficult verses in the Bible. Its meaning has been pondered and debated by theologians almost since the very beginning of Christianity, and understanding it correctly remains one of the greatest challenges to our faith. Who or what is the Word? And what does it mean to say that the Word was 'with God' and at the same time, God also?

John himself was in no doubt that the Word was to be identified with Jesus Christ, because a few lines further down, he adds that 'the Word became flesh and dwelt among us', making it quite clear that someone or something divine had become a human being. But was this Word a 'person' before becoming human, or just a part of God, like his mind, for instance? Or are we really talking about a divine plan, which was brought to fulfilment in the life of Jesus, who was himself no more than a man?

These questions matter, because the answers which we give to them will determine what we go on to say about the life and ministry of Jesus himself. Was the prophet of

Nazareth just an extraordinary rabbi who introduced a new understanding of Judaism to his followers, and paid the price for it? Or was he God in human flesh, using his time on earth as a preparation for his death and resurrection, which would accomplish his great work of saving the human race? The first of these views could be held by almost anybody without making any real difference to them, or to anyone else. It is the second option which causes problems, because it demands a level of belief which goes beyond the merely human, and which, once it is embraced, will change a person's life for ever. It is the second belief which created the Christian Church, and which continues to produce new believers today. Without it, there would be no Christians, and no Christianity. This is why it matters, and why we have to come to grips with it before we consider anything else about the life and work of the man Jesus of Nazareth.

What Christians believe is this. There is one God, who has revealed himself to mankind in a number of different ways. When he created the world, he spoke to our first ancestors through the laws of nature, which they could understand and accept as the gift of the one who had made them. Later on, he spoke through prophets, who were inspired to preach a double message – of condemnation, and of redemption. The condemnation came because men had sinned against God, and departed from what they knew was right. But God was not willing to abandon his creatures, and alongside the condemnation there was a message of redemption through sacrifice and death. This was accomplished by a series of elaborate rituals, centred on the temple which God commanded to be built for him at Jerusalem. But it was always understood that this was a provisional solution to the problem, because one day God would intervene in a more decisive manner, and bring to perfection what was only indicated by signs and symbols in the temple. This work of fulfilment came about in Jesus, who put an end to the need for the temple sacrifices, and opened up a completely new understanding and experience of God.

But although the God who did all this was one and unique in himself, this oneness was not as simple as we might imagine. In a sense, the oneness of God could be compared to the oneness of the atom, the smallest thing which can have an independent existence. Atoms appear to be one on the outside, and so they are, but scientists have discovered that *inside* the atom there is a whole world of energy, represented by protons, neutrons and electrons, which cannot be detected independently, but which constitute the atom and which, if the atom is somehow split, will release an energy which might be powerful enough to destroy huge chunks of our planet. In a somewhat similar way, God appears to be one on the outside, but inside him there are three persons, who relate to each other and who jointly do the work of God in the world. These persons do not exist independently of each other, but neither are they separate parts of God in the way that protons, for instance, are parts of the atom. Each person is fully God in himself, but no one person exists on his own. To know one of them is to know all three.

In the Old Testament, God revealed himself in his

oneness, without any distinction of persons being visible at that time. Many people automatically assume that this God can be identified with the person of the Father, as he is revealed in the New Testament, but this is not strictly accurate. Before the coming of Christ, all three persons spoke with one voice, and it is impossible to say whether one of them is more obviously present than the others or not. We have to remember that when Jesus taught his disciples to pray 'Our Father', he was saying something which struck them as quite new, and when he called God *his* Father, he scandalised the Jews who listened to him (John 5:18). So characteristic was this of Jesus, that even many years later, the Aramaic word *Abba* ('Father') which he used in prayer was still remembered and employed as a reminder of the uniqueness of the Christian experience (Gal. 4:6). This would not have been the case if the Jews had been accustomed to use the word 'Father' in their prayers, so we must assume that they did not normally think of God in that way.

As the Jews who objected to Jesus' use of the word 'Father' so clearly saw, to call God that was to claim a relationship with him which was fundamentally a relationship between equals. A son may show his father deference, and accept that he has a certain historical and even logical priority, but it is obvious that he is equal to his father at the basic human level. Indeed, it is not uncommon for fathers to be so proud of their children that they almost make them better than themselves, if only because their children have been able to achieve things which they have been denied. Certainly, no-one would ever suggest that a child can be compared to a dog or a cat, which really are inferior beings.

By calling God his Father, Jesus was telling everybody that he was also God, an assertion which was bound to cause problems if the people who heard this believed that there was (and could be) only one God. How was it possible for a Father and a Son to share the same unique being? The New Testament does not give a specific answer to this question, but there are a number of important indications which help us understand how this might be so. John indicates that the Word was there in the beginning, so that there could never have been a time when the Word did not exist. This Word was 'with God', which means not only that the Word existed inside the being of God long before the world was created, but that the Word could be distinguished in some way as a distinct entity. Finally, the Word was God in the full sense of the term, so that whatever was said about the one would automatically apply to the other as well. The Bible nowhere uses the word 'person' to describe the Word, or to describe God either, for that matter. Yet it is clear from what the Bible does say that the term 'person' is an appropriate one to express what the Bible means. Persons are not things – we must use the words 'he' or 'she' to describe them, not the word 'it'. The Bible always refers to God as 'he', and therefore the Word, being God, must be a 'he' also. Equally important, John tells us that the Word did the same things which God did at the beginning of the world – 'through him all things were made, and without him was not anything made, which was made'. This rather convoluted sentence makes it plain that the Word must be regarded as our creator, and this theme was later taken up by the Apostle Paul, who said much the same thing in his letter to the Colossians (Col. 1:16-17).

If the Word is our creator, this means that we cannot define him in terms which apply only to the created order. This is important when it comes to deciding what is meant by the word 'Son', when this is applied to the Word. The Father-Son imagery which we have already remarked on normally implies that there was a process of birth, and that the father existed for quite some time before the son appeared on the scene. But in the case of the Word, this assumption does not apply, because the Word was there in the beginning, so we have to understand the Father-Son imagery in a different way.

For many centuries after the controversies in the early Church period, this question was seldom discussed, but modern feminism has raised an entirely new dimension of the issue. Is God male? What does the use of masculine imagery mean? First of all, we can say with complete assurance that God is not male, at least not in the normal human sense. Furthermore, anything to do with the process of birth and reproduction must be firmly excluded from our consideration of him. Father and Son are intended to express something about the relationship which exists between these two persons, which may be paralleled at the human level, but which is not determined by it. The two persons are like each other, and the Son is explicitly described as the 'heir' of everything which the Father possesses. Their relationship is not one of competition or dominance, but of mutual fulfilment and interdependence. Could the same thing be equally well expressed by a Mother-Daughter analogy, or even a Husband-Wife one?

The main problem with a Mother-Daughter image is that it would introduce a sexual element which does not belong in God. The Daughter could easily be thought of as dwelling inside the Mother's womb before being given birth. Something like this was actually believed by a number of early Christians, who imagined that the Word was somehow hidden inside God until he was produced in order to create the world. The result was a degree of confusion about the Word's identity, which at one extreme led Arius (d. 336) to claim that he was a creature, and not the creator. A Mother-Daughter image would only reinforce that possibility, and therefore it is less suitable as a description of God's inner being. Then again, a Mother-Daughter image would make the incarnation of the Daughter impossible unless the Mother also became incarnate and allowed herself to be impregnated by a man. This would obviously go against what the Bible says about the Father's invisibility and transcendence, and would run the risk of turning Christianity into a fertility cult – something which would not have been impossible in the ancient world, however odd it may seem nowadays.

A Husband-Wife analogy is also inappropriate, because it puts the emphasis on complementarity, which is based on diversity, not on similarity. That is extremely important and creative at the human level, but it is fundamentally different from God. Father and Son are both complete in themselves, and do not need one another in order to be creative. That is important, because it reminds us that everything which God has done he has done of his own free will, and not in order to fulfil any necessity inside himself. It may seem strange to say that God has no need of us, but that is true, and what is more, it is essential. Our disobedience cannot diminish God in any way, even if he wants us to live with him in eternity and share in his work of creating and controlling the universe. Our relationship with God is not based on some need inside him, but on his love for us – a love which is fully realised in the eternal relationship between the Father and the Son.

It is the Bible's assertion that 'God is love' (1 John 4:16) which provides the true framework for our understanding of the pre-existence of Christ. Love is not a thing, with an objective existence of its own. For love to mean anything at all, there has to be a person who can love and another person who can receive that love. Furthermore, true love has to be mutual for it to be truly perfect. It is possible to have one-sided love, and there are many examples of this in our experience. Parents often love their children and sacrifice themselves for them, without receiving any comparable love in return. Men love women, and women love men, without being loved back. But in each of these cases, and others as well, the result is tragic. To reject love, for whatever reason, is to cause hurt and division. If the Son did not love the Father with the same intensity as the Father loves him there would be an imbalance in the Godhead which would be destructive of the unity of God. This is clearly out of the question, and so we can say with some assurance that 'God is love' is the ultimate guarantee that the Father and the Son are equal to each other in every respect.

It is sometimes asked whether we can say that the Son of God appeared to the prophets of the Old Testament before he became incarnate as Jesus of Nazareth. Many Christians have believed this, and have quoted such incidents as the appearance of angels to different Old Testament characters as evidence in favour of this hypothesis. The argument goes something like this. The Son clearly exists in eternity, and was therefore present in God throughout the Old Testament period. When the prophets saw angels, they frequently said that they had met with God himself. But the New Testament teaches us that only in Christ has God become visible, so on that basis, it appears that if the prophets did see God, it must have been Christ whom they saw. Finally, there are some indications in the New Testament that Christ was indeed present with believers before his coming. When the children of Israel were wandering through the desert, for example, they were accompanied by a rock which gave them life-giving water, and the Apostle Paul tells us that 'the rock was Christ' (1 Cor. 10:4).

Statements of this kind have been enough for many people to conclude that the Son did in fact appear to various Old Testament characters, even if he was not recognised by them as such. There is no way that we can say that they are wrong, because we do not have any evidence which would disprove this claim. So it has to be admitted that these Christians may well have been right.

On the other hand, there is no evidence to prove this either. The writer to the Hebrews says a lot about the Old Testament, and mentions even fairly obscure people like Melchizedek, who was a prototype of the Christ who was to come, but he never says anything about pre-incarnational appearances of Christ himself. Had there been any, it seems only logical to suppose that he would have made the most of them, but he did not do so. In his great list of the Old Testament saints, he concludes with the remark that, in spite of all the spiritual blessings which they enjoyed, they did not receive the great blessing which has been given to us as Christians. And of course, he begins his epistle with the remark that whereas God had spoken in many different ways to the prophets, he has spoken to us in the Son, a statement which would seem to make it clear that Christ did not appear before his incarnation, even though he was present and active in the Godhead.

Finally, there is another reason why it is unlikely that the Son of God appeared before his incarnation. This is because of what we have already said about knowing God on the 'inside'. The big difference between Jews and Christians is that Jews know God on the 'outside'. They see him in his oneness but are most deeply impressed by his holiness, or separation from us. In the Old Testament this is reinforced in many different ways. When Moses met with God in the burning bush, he had to remove his shoes, because he was standing on holy ground. The Israelites could not touch the ark of the covenant, and those who did so were struck dead. In the temple, God dwelt in the holy of holies, where only the high priest could enter – and then only once a year. But as Christians, we are seated in the heavenly places in Christ (Eph. 2:6), and have *access* to the Father through him (Eph. 2:18). The barriers which existed before have now been broken down, and we have an experience of God which was not known to those who came before Christ, however close they may have been to him in other ways.

So we must conclude that the Son of God has always existed with the Father, that he is our creator just as much as the Father is, and that in his incarnation he revealed both himself and the Father to us. It is to that revelation, its meaning and its consequences that we must now turn.

2

The Annunciation
(Luke 1: 26–37)

The story of the annunciation appears in only one Gospel, (though there it takes up thirteen verses), and its absence from the other three is matched by an indifference to the event which is fairly widespread in the Reformed churches. Until 1751, the Feast of the Annunciation, fixed on 25 March so as to come exactly nine months before Christmas, was counted as the beginning of the calendar year, because the incarnation of Jesus was held to have begun at the moment of his conception in the womb of Mary. But since then it has fallen into almost total oblivion, remembered only as an appendage to the Christmas story which might be used to heighten the mysterious quality of the Nativity. Ignoring the annunciation, however, is an open invitation to denying the virgin birth of Christ, since without it we are left to conclude that Jesus was born by ordinary means, and therefore was not God in human flesh. There are even people who have claimed that the story of the annunciation was invented at least partly in order to cover up the 'fact' that Mary conceived her Son out of wedlock!

Of course, this ignorance and scepticism is found only in Protestant churches. Roman Catholics have never abandoned their awareness of the annunciation as a distinct event with its own theological significance. On the contrary, as many Protestants have declined into an unbelieving liberalism, the Roman church has gone off in the opposite direction and placed enormous emphasis on the Virgin Mary. The story of the annunciation is the rather slender basis which it has found in Scripture for its doctrine of Mary's immaculate conception (proclaimed as dogma in 1854), and from there it was but a short step to a belief in her physical assumption into heaven (proclaimed as dogma in 1950). Because of all this, the place of Mary in Christian teaching is a subject which cannot be avoided when the annunciation is being considered. It may be true that some modern Roman Catholics have recoiled from the extreme forms of Mariolatry which are canonised in shrines like Lourdes, but this has not affected the church's teaching, and in many parts of the world, Catholic devotion to Mary remains strong. To date the question has not surfaced much in ecumenical dialogue, but it can hardly remain submerged for ever. Sooner or later we shall have to face the problem squarely, and Protestants will be obliged to give an account of their own understanding of Mary's role in the salvation of the world.

For this reason it is necessary to look carefully at the story as it is written in Luke's Gospel, and examine what its theological and Mariological implications are. As a first point, it is worth bearing in mind that Luke placed Mary's visitation alongside the story of the birth of John the Baptist.

It was clearly Luke's intention to relate the two events, since not only are Mary and Elizabeth described as kinswomen, but the first three months of Mary's pregnancy overlap with the last three of Elizabeth's, a period which the two women spent together (v. 56). More important still, the foetus of John the Baptist leapt in the womb at the approach of Mary, not because of her, but because of the Child whom she was carrying. Elizabeth understood this by means of a special revelation which was given to her, and she gave expression to her experience by referring to Mary as 'the mother of my Lord' (v. 43), a nice touch which indicates that she knew that it was God himself who had entered Mary's womb to be born.

There is a certain parallel between the two women, in that both had experienced a miraculous conception, but beyond that, the differences between them are more important than any similarities. Elizabeth's pregnancy was of a type familiar from the Old Testament, and belongs in that context. It was abnormal in that she was old and barren, but the process of conception, as in the cases of Isaac and Samuel, followed the usual human pattern. The child she eventually gave birth to was fully human, and in no sense divine, although he was called to an extraordinary ministry, just as Samuel had been. With Mary though, the situation was quite different. She was young (possibly no more than twelve or thirteen) and potentially fertile, on the threshold of married life. We must also bear in mind that fact that, whereas Elizabeth's pregnancy had 'taken away her shame', Mary's had done the exact opposite – it had brought reproach and potential disgrace on a woman who had never known a man (Matt. 1:19).

In the conception of Jesus, the Holy Spirit not only violated the laws of nature in a way which is essentially different from what he did in his earlier miracles, but he also seems to have disregarded public feelings of morality, as Matthew did not fail to point out (Matt. 1:18-19). In working out his purpose for our salvation, God demonstrated his sovereignty right from the start, not only over nature but over the requirements of the Law as well. It was a demonstration of his power which was to become a hallmark of the ministry of Jesus, provoking both wonder and scandal in the minds of those who could perhaps have accepted a miracle, but who could never have agreed to set aside the commandments of God as they understood them.

Why did God behave in this way? One of the reasons must surely be that obedience is the keynote of the life of faith, even when that obedience goes against the customs of the time. It is easy to confuse this with antinomianism, or breaking the law for the sake of it, but this is not at all what was happening in Mary's case. The Old Testament prophets had often been commanded to say and do things which went against expectations, even things which in another context would have been wrong, as when Hosea was told to go out and marry a prostitute (against his own will). There was scriptural warrant for the birth of the Messiah from a virgin (Isa. 7:14), so the idea cannot have come as a complete surprise. Yet how difficult it can be to apply God's commands in the hard world of practice! Mary must have known that she had everything to lose, in human terms, if she obeyed the angel's voice. Her submission took great courage. It was not an antinomian gesture of defiance, but a humble acceptance of the Spirit's purpose, in spite of those like Joseph, who were more troubled by the demands of the letter of the Law. Antinomianism is rebellion for the sake of self-gratification, whereas Mary's action was one of submission in a spirit of self-sacrifice.

To proclaim his intentions, God used the angel Gabriel, who was a familiar figure in the angelic world. It was Gabriel who appeared to Zechariah (v. 19), and he was also mentioned in the book of Daniel (8:16; 9:21). Furthermore, he was one of the four archangels named in the book of Enoch, which shows that his importance was widely recognised in Jewish circles generally. We are not told why he should have been entrusted with this mission, although in Daniel he is described as having the form of a man, and in his appearance to Zechariah he says that he stands in the presence of God (v. 19). It may be that as these two characteristics are typical of the glorified Christ, God chose him as the most suitable emissary to announce his great work to Mary. But we cannot be sure, because, in his conversation with Mary, the archangel does not speak of himself. His one purpose is to inform Mary of *her* calling, and to explain in some measure what that was to involve.

It is perhaps worth recalling that there is a great concentration of significant Old Testament names in these few verses. Names had an importance in biblical times

The Annunciation

which is hard to imagine nowadays, and one of the main purposes of the annunciation was to reveal the name of Jesus (v. 31). This corresponds to the Old Testament Joshua, a fact which can hardly have been accidental, although its meaning is not explained in the text. In the space of a few verses, moreover, we are reminded of Joseph, David, Jacob and Miriam (Mary). It would probably be stretching the evidence to read anything into the names of Joseph and Mary, though it is at least interesting to note that both are linked to the time of bondage in Egypt. The name of Joshua must certainly be associated with deliverance from the bondage of sin, because the typological link between Egypt and the unregenerate life is too strong a theme in Scripture to be ignored.

However, it is important to notice that Moses is nowhere mentioned in this connection. Jesus came, not to emulate his work, but that of his successor, who led the house of Jacob out of the wilderness into the Promised Land. The never-ending kingdom which the angel Gabriel promised to Mary's Son is the New Testament equivalent of this Promised Land, which Jesus would rule because he was of the house and lineage of King David, the man to whom the original inheritance was bequeathed.

Jesus was the inheritor of the promises made to David, an important point which would cause considerable speculation and confusion during his later ministry. His disciples (and others too) thought that he would be a secular ruler along the lines of Herod the Great, who also feared this possibility (Matt. 2:3). But the kingdom of Jesus was not of this world, just as his descent from David was not of this world either. For note that it is nowhere stated that Mary was a descendant of David, but rather Joseph, who was not Jesus' father. It was therefore by a legal contract of marriage, not by blood descent, that Jesus would claim this inheritance. Joseph was not merely an accessory to the event, designed to give it respectability in the world's eyes. He too, had a role to play, as the one who conferred historical and prophetic legitimacy, along with legal paternity, on the infant in Mary's womb.

This is important, because it brings out the fact that the eternal reign of Christ is not dependent on his birth from Mary. The Catholic tendency to describe her as Queen of Heaven is implicitly denied in Scripture, where the royal inheritance is expressly stated to have come through his human stepfather, not his mother.

The most contentious verse however is verse 28, where Gabriel describes Mary as 'highly favoured'. This translation of the Greek word *kecharitomene* is undoubtedly designed to offset the all too familiar Latin of the Vulgate, *gratia plena* ('full of grace'), which has been used to support the most extravagant claims on Mary's behalf. We need not quarrel with Jerome over his translation, given that Latin is a less subtle language than Greek and has little choice of expression. We may also admit, on the Protestant side, that 'highly favoured' could obscure the word 'grace' (Greek: *charis*, which is undoubtedly present in *kecharitomene*). To say that Mary was 'graced', though, would sound rather odd in modern English, and could easily convey the impression that she had been covered over with a superficial layer of something called 'grace', or even that she had been forgiven for something she had never done.

Nevertheless, there is a real difficulty with *gratia plena* which cannot be ignored. Roman Catholic theology has treated the Vulgate as equal to the original text for doctrinal purposes, and has gone on from there to describe Mary as sinless from birth, as co-redemptrix of the human race, and even as co-mediatrix in heaven! But there is no way in which it is possible to interpret *kecharitomene* like that. Mary was a recipient of grace, not a potential *dispenser* of it. Furthermore the context makes it clear that she received God's grace for a particular purpose, which was to give birth to the Son. Nowhere is there any suggestion that the divine favour may have exempted her from the need of salvation, or that it placed her on a level of near-equality with the Saviour in relation to the world!

At a deeper level of course, we are confronted here with the whole meaning of *grace*. The word indicates an activity of God in the heart of man which he can only *receive* in a spirit of humble acceptance, because by its very nature grace is quite undeserved. God's grace may impel us to action, as in the process of sanctification, but human beings cannot co-operate with God in a way which would make us contributors to our own salvation. It is this issue which lies at the heart of the debate. Mary may serve as a *model* for Christians, in that she responded obediently to the call of God, but in no way can she claim *superiority* over them.

Something of this is in fact hinted at in verse 29. Mary's

reaction to the angel was one of disturbed surprise. Had she been 'full of grace' and sinless from the womb, she would presumably have known how to cope with what would hardly have been an unexpected situation. Instead we find her amazed and upset, as any young girl would be in a similar position. The angel had to calm her fears, by repeating that she had found favour with God, before informing her of the service which she was destined to perform. Furthermore, she was promised nothing for herself; it was *he* who would be called great, the Son of the Most High.

It is much easier to interpret this text as an example of how a Christian ought to respond to God than as the testimony of a woman so full of grace that she could not sin. Her troubled state is one which is common to many Christians, when they are called to a particular form of service for God. Which of us is sufficient for the task? How can we ever claim such a familiarity with the ways of God, that his work in our lives should never take us by surprise? Do we not see here a typical example of what happens to so many men and women who are called? In this respect, Mary is closer to Jeremiah (Jer. 1:6) than to Jesus, whose obedience to his Father was of a different order altogether.

Finally, we must not leave the story of the annunciation without considering what it tells us about the work of the Trinity in the conception of Jesus. When Gabriel explains to Mary what will happen to her he says that the Holy Spirit will come upon her, and that the power of the Most High will overshadow her, so that the fruit of her womb will be the Son of God. Here we catch a glimpse of the three Persons of the Trinity working together to bring about the miracle of the incarnation. It is possible that 'the power of the Most High' is meant to be an alternative and parallel way of referring to the Holy Spirit, but even so, it merely emphasizes that he is the agent of the Most High, who in verse 32 is plainly equated with the Father. The point is not a trivial one, because the incarnation was a work of God in the fulness of his Trinitarian being. We must never suppose that the Son *left* the other Persons behind, nor that the incarnation caused any division in, or deduction from, the Godhead. The Son came to earth in order that we, in our fellowship with him, might know something of his fellowship with the Father and the Spirit, and thus share with them in the Trinitarian life of God. This too, is part of the message of the annunciation, and we must hold fast to it even as we contemplate the miracle of divine conception in the womb of God's servant Mary.

3

The Incarnation

The incarnation belongs to the inner circle of Christian teaching. It is part of that precious store of doctrine which shapes the whole of our Christian life and penetrates beyond it to bear witness, even in our secular society, of the abiding truths of the gospel. Christmas, the great feast of the incarnation, is the most popular holiday of the year; it has even spread, thanks to commercialism, to non-Christian countries like Japan. At the theological level, the activities of the 'Jesus seminar' and its equivalents remind us of the importance which the doctrine still has in contemporary theological debate. Somewhere in between these two extremes, a host of voices calls us to practise a more 'incarnational' faith, which usually means a modified form of that social gospel which passed for liberalism in the 1920s.

At every level of the Church, the incarnation is now being debated, perhaps more than any other single doctrine. In the Scriptures it is spoken of somewhat indirectly in the Gospels of Matthew and Luke. It can also be found in Philippians 2:5-11, in Colossians and in Hebrews, not to mention in half a dozen or so other passages. Yet by common consent, both in the ancient Church and in modern times, the main focus of theological speculation is the Fourth Gospel, in particular its famous Prologue, and especially the words of John 1:14 – *the Word became flesh*. John's expression is at once both arrestingly direct and tantalizingly obscure. What can it mean to say that the Word, which is surely an intangible thing, became *flesh*?

The need for caution in interpreting this verse is reinforced when we remember that the Christological disputes of the early centuries, which culminated in the famous (though now much-maligned) definition of the Council of Chalcedon (451), can largely be understood as an attempt to expound this verse correctly. For Athanasius (c. 296-373), it was the key to Christology, and his views were appealed to by later generations as the irreproachable source of orthodoxy. Between the first council of Nicaea (325) and the council of Chalcedon, an entire theological system was built on the polarity between Word and flesh, which, with minor modifications in the interests of greater clarity, remains the touchstone of right belief even today.

The extent to which this is accepted is demonstrated by the furore which is caused every time it is asserted that the incarnation is a 'myth'. Those who claim this know they will cause a fuss, because at grassroots level, Christological orthodoxy remains as strong as ever. But such disputes also tend to show that many believers have a faith in the incarnation which is more passive than active, more traditional than vital. To attack it might be sacrilege, but to defend it coherently and adequately is a task beyond the reach (and, if the truth be told, outside the interests) of many of those who are scandalised. As with so many of the familiar landmarks of faith, the importance of the incarnation is sensed and accepted without being fully understood. All too often, what Christ *did* on the cross remains more immediately important than who he was, even though the former depends entirely on the latter for its meaning and effectiveness.

It is always easier to tell a story than to explain a concept, and the incarnation has been one of the chief sufferers from this tendency. At Christmas, when the doctrine can hardly be avoided, a nativity play staged by the Sunday school can always squeeze out a sermon, and the casual churchgoers who appear in the pews do not want to be shaken out of their carolling sentimentality into serious intellectual argument. During the festive season, the incarnation is smothered in pious sentimentality, and the Church allows its doctrinal foundation to be eroded by ignorant folklore.

To resist the prevailing trend is never easy, but in this case it must surely be attempted. In the Book of Common Prayer, the Epistle and Gospel for Christmas Day are Hebrews 1 and John 1 respectively – a clear reminder that the purpose of celebration is rooted, not in a manger at Bethlehem, but in the eternal plan of God, now made manifest in Christ, the fulness of the divine revelation to men. We are not dealing here with an accident, or with something which is basically no more than a rather unusual event. The incarnation of Christ is a moment of the deepest spiritual and historical significance. God, who 'at sundry times and in divers manners' had spoken to the ancients by the prophets, now *in these last days* has spoken to us in his Son. The coming of Christ is the beginning of the final act of God's saving work – the *last days* are upon us, signalled not by the current threat of nuclear destruction but by the birth of Jesus Christ, the Son of God! The terror of judgement and the promise of redemption come together in this, the final visitation of God to his people.

When God chose to become man, we note that he did so as the Word. Much has been written about this Logos of God, and we know that the Greek term can mean *mind, thought* and *reason* even more readily than 'word' (which in Greek is *lexis*. But, however we translate it, we cannot escape the simple fact that the Logos appears as an intellectual, somewhat abstract reality. Many scholars have equated it with Platonic or Stoic concepts of a Supreme Mind, and this has led to the accusation that both the Johannine Prologue and the doctrine of the incarnation are manifestations of a Hellenistic intrusion into the realms of Christian piety.

In responding to this, it is not necessary to examine every argument in detail; it is sufficient to note that what *happened* to the Logos, the fact that he became flesh makes a Greek philosophical influence impossible. It is a basic axiom of every Greek school of philosophy that the spiritual and material realms do not mix. Even Stoicism, which held that spirit was a highly refined form of matter, could not countenance such a change. In any case, Greek philosophy thought primarily in terms of *nature(s)*, which means that for the Logos to have become 'flesh' would imply a chemical transformation of the divine essence into human flesh. Such a transformation, even if it were possible, would mean the extinction of the Logos as a separate entity, rather in the way that the transformation of a caterpillar into a butterfly 'destroys' the former. Once such a change had taken place in the Logos, it would have been impossible to behold his glory, as the text says the disciples did. There is therefore no reason at all to suppose that the text reflects a philosophical influence of any kind.

In fact, as the fathers of the Church saw, the Incarnation cannot be explained in terms of *nature*. In Christ there are two natures, as the Chalcedonian Definition affirmed, which are 'without confusion and without change'. Each nature, the divine and the human, retains its own properties intact, with no infringement on or by the other. The union, and thus the *became* of John 1:14, can only be understood in terms of *person*. The Word is not a thing, but the Son of God, the second Person of the Trinity. In becoming flesh, this Person took to himself a human nature, not by divesting himself of his divinity, which he could not do, but by adding to himself a second nature – 'taking the manhood into God' in the words of the Athanasian Creed.

In this context, 'flesh' means the created human nature of Adam. It must be understood that of itself, the flesh is neither sinful nor sinning. It is true that Jesus came 'in the likeness of sinful flesh' (Rom. 8:3), but this means, not that he was a sinner, but that he possessed the same basic human nature as the first Adam who sinned. This was a necessity, since without this he could not have become sin for us on the cross. The point is that sin is not a category which can be applied to any natural thing simply on the basis of its being part of creation. Sin is a personal act of disobedience, which in Adam produced that broken relationship with God (our 'fallen state') which every human being has inherited. When the New Testament uses the word *flesh* to describe man in this fallen state, the term has a spiritual and not a physical meaning.

John 1:14 also uses the word in a spiritual sense, as is apparent from the following line: 'we beheld his glory'. At the purely natural level, it would have been quite impossible for anyone to behold the glory of the Word in the human flesh of Jesus. We know this from the Gospels. Jesus grew up in Nazareth, but when he began to preach his own village rejected him – they had known him all his life, and it was quite clear to them that his pretensions to be a prophet and teacher could not possibly be true. Nicodemus recognised that he was 'a teacher come from God' because of the miracles he performed, but that was still a far cry from beholding his glory, as Jesus himself was at pains to point out.

When recognition came, as it did in the case of Peter, Jesus himself made it clear that this was not natural knowledge which any clever person might discern, but a special revelation from God (Matt. 16:17). To behold the glory of the Word was a privilege granted to few, and we must never forget that those few were men and women who had been touched by the Spirit of God.

Peter's confession, and even more the implication contained in the past tense of *beheld*, must bring us to what is perhaps the most frequent question Christians ask about the incarnation. Were the disciples specially privileged to see the Son of God in human flesh? Did they have an experience of him which must forever be denied to those of us who follow after? How often do we imagine that our doubts and fears as believers would never exist if we had the Master with us in the way the disciples did! Certainly it must be admitted that it was a great privilege to live with Jesus, and we must never forget the importance of this for the subsequent witness of the apostles. When the time came for them to choose a successor to the traitor Judas, they insisted on a man who had known Jesus from the beginning of his ministry (Acts 1:21-22). The Gospels themselves are eye-witness accounts of the events they describe, and no one would question their special place, even within the inspired Scriptures. Yet these same Gospels offer us the greatest reassurance we need, that this imagined superiority of the disciples' experience has no basis in fact. As far as the spiritual perception of the disciples is concerned, the Gospels are a rather discouraging record of failure – the failure to understand Jesus' teaching, the failure to obey his commands, the disloyalty of Peter and the others at the trial and crucifixion. This is hardly the behaviour we would expect from men who had beheld the glory of the Son of God! These men may be set apart from us in one sense, but they are like us in a way which we cannot fail to recognise as the authentic experience of every believer.

Why should this be so? The answer lies not so much in the basic sinfulness of the apostles, though of course that must never be forgotten, as in the glory of the Word, which comes to us as it did to them. Jesus Christ is no longer present with us in the flesh, but the meaning of John 1:14 goes deeper than this. For the verse does not speak of the Man of Nazareth, but of the eternal Word, which immediately links the text with the great theme of revelation.

The Word of God which became flesh in Jesus Christ has also, in a different way, become paper and ink in the words of the Bible. The Holy Scriptures are the Voice of God to the Church, the Word inscripturated. As Christians we need to understand that the Bible performs for us the same function as the incarnate body of the Son of God performed for the disciples. In other words, our doctrine of Scripture is not a philosophical abstraction based on some essentially pagan notion of 'inspiration', but an offshoot of our Christology. The same teaching which is applied to Christ can and must be applied to the Bible as well. Christ is one divine Person in two natures – divine and human. So also, the Bible is one divine Voice in two natures, one divine and the other human. These two natures are not separated or cut off from one another, but neither are they mixed or confused together. They are united by the Divine Voice, which speaks to us in and through the text.

Furthermore, just as the revelation of Christ's divinity was a gift of God and not the result of human investigation, so the recognition of the Scriptures as the

Word of God can only come by the witness of the Spirit. Calvin saw this clearly when he said that it was the inner witness of the Holy Spirit which assures us of the truth of the Bible, though it seems that he never tied his insight in this matter to his Christology, at least not explicitly. Today, of course, we see this truth in the work of unbelieving biblical scholars. Like Satan who tried to tempt Jesus into revealing his glory in the wrong way, these men play with the Scriptures in a forlorn attempt to tease out its secrets. They find nothing of course, any more than a doctor would have found some sign of divinity if he had examined the entrails of the man Jesus. To those who are deprived of the eye of faith, the Bible can never be more than a human book, however important it may be in the history of human culture.

Today it is in the Bible that we behold the glory of the Word. If we have not grasped the teaching of Jesus at this point – 'the Scriptures speak of me' (John 5:39) – we have not begun to read the Bible with the mind of Christ. To put it another way, we have not begun to consider the importance of the incarnation for us today. The belief that it is the Church, as the 'body of Christ' which is the historical continuation of the incarnate Christ is attractive to many, but it is an idea which lacks scriptural support. As Augustine observed, Christ's body is in Heaven, and where the head is, there the members must be also. The more liberal view, that a Spirit-filled human Jesus is the archetype of the life of self-sacrifice and morality demanded of his followers, is also attractive to many, but in the end it is no more than wishful thinking. Those who beheld his glory were conscious of the gulf which separated him from them – there was no possibility of merely human imitation here. When Peter tried to walk on water he failed miserably, and was rebuked for his lack of faith. He evidently saw the imitation of Christ in purely human terms, and sank as a result.

The incarnation retains its importance for us as a living truth, (as opposed to its historical importance for the unfolding of God's plan of salvation), because it confirms the Scriptures and tells us how to understand them. How often are we told that Jesus did something or other, in order that 'the Scriptures might be fulfilled'. How often do we find in the Gospels words of Christ which point to the true meaning of the Bible, which is nothing less than the revelation of his message and the account of his work?

This is the main importance of the incarnation for us at the practical level. By his Spirit who unfolds the teaching of the Bible, the Word of God continues to dwell among us today! God grant that in the power of that Spirit we too might behold his glory, and in the pages of Scripture discern the Voice of the One who is the only-begotten Son of the Father.

4

The Baptism of Jesus
(Matthew 3:13-17; Mark 1:9-13;
Luke 3:21-22; John 1:29-34)

The baptism of Jesus was the beginning of his earthly ministry, and it is the only incident in his life, apart from the events surrounding his death, which is mentioned in all four Gospels. This in itself would command our attention, but his baptism is important for a number of other reasons as well. For a start, it was not necessary. We are baptised for the forgiveness of our sins, but Jesus did not have any sins which needed to be forgiven. He was baptised in order to fulfil all righteousness, which in the context means the Old Testament law, but baptism was not an Old Testament practice. He had already been circumcised when he was eight days old, and when he was twelve he had gone up to Jerusalem for his bar-mitzvah, so from the Jewish point of view, he was already a member in good standing of the covenant community. Baptism, in so far as it was practised at all, seems to have been reserved for Gentile converts to Judaism, who were baptised in order to symbolise the fact that their conversion had purified them from the taint of the world's sins. Within Judaism, the only sign of baptism seems to have been in the ministry of his cousin John, who was called 'the Baptist' precisely because of this oddity. John baptised for repentance, and as a sign of the coming of the kingdom of God, but he was the first to recognise, as John's account reminds us, that his ministry had nothing to offer Jesus. So what was going on, and what lessons do we learn from it?

The first thing which has to be said is that the baptism of Jesus cannot be compared with the baptism of Christians. This is not just because Jesus received the baptism of John, which is not identical with the baptism practised by the Church. More importantly, Jesus' baptism could not possibly have had the same meaning as ours, because his spiritual condition and relationship to God were completely different. It cannot be stressed too often that Jesus was not a Christian – and could not have been. A Christian is a sinner who is saved by the grace of God given to him because of his faith in the shed blood of Christ. But Jesus was not a sinner, he did not die to save himself, and it makes no sense to say that he 'believed' in what he had done. But in spite of this, there is a strong tendency in the Christian Church to behave as though Jesus was indeed the first (and greatest) Christian.

One of the earliest of whom we have some knowledge was a man called Paul of Samosata, who was bishop of Antioch from 260 to 272. In 268 he was condemned by a synod in that city, which accused him of the heresy we know as 'adoptionism'. Apparently, Paul believed that Jesus was an ordinary man, with a human father, who was adopted by God at the time of his baptism. When Jesus went down into the water, the heavens opened and a dove descended on him, as the voice of God proclaimed that now he was his 'beloved Son'. Paul's motive for saying this was probably pastoral. He wanted to explain the importance of Christian baptism as the ceremony in which we become children of God. If baptism is the sign of our spiritual adoption, and Jesus was baptised, then it seemed obvious to Paul that Jesus was also adopted as the Son of God. He probably did not put it quite like this, but the effect was to turn Jesus into the first Christian, a model for us to follow.

Now the Bible does say that we are to be imitators of Christ (1 Cor. 11:1), so there must be some way in which our lives are meant to parallel his. Why should this not begin with baptism? Of course, in some sense it does, because baptism is the beginning of our Christian life, and therefore also the beginning of our imitation of Christ. But while all this is true, we cannot conclude that Jesus' baptism (or his subsequent ministry) are in any way similar to ours. Quite apart from the reasons already given, which have to do with Jesus' fundamental sinlessness, there is the other side which has to be remembered, which is that Jesus came for a specific purpose, which was to die for the sins of the world. This purpose is made very clear at the time of his baptism, when he is hailed by John as 'the Lamb of God, who takes away the sins of the world' (John 1:29). However much we may be called to be like Jesus, even to the point of taking up our cross and following him, we are not called to die for the sins of others, nor could we do so even if we wanted to. Jesus' life and ministry were unique, and therefore the baptism which began that ministry was unique also.

Why was Jesus baptised? The first reason was that it was a way of validating the ministry of John the Baptist. John was his distant cousin, and the connection between the two men went back to their birth, as Luke reminds us in the first chapter of his Gospel. John was six months older than Jesus, a time difference which was meant to symbolise both their closeness and the fact that John was the 'forerunner', who came into the world in order to prepare the way for the coming of the Messiah. When he grew to adulthood, he went into the desert country of the Jordan River valley, where he practised baptism as the key to his message of repentance in preparation for the great work of God which was about to come. Today we know that John was by no means as unusual as he may appear to be in the New Testament account.

The Jewish people had only recently lost their political independence, and come under Roman rule. There was a sense that a spiritual crisis was looming, because Roman society, for all its tolerance, was basically assimilationist. Unlike other peoples in ancient times, the Romans were prepared to grant their citizenship to foreigners, and this could include even Jews. The spread of Greek ideas and culture following the conquests of Alexander the Great (d. 323 BC) had already created a situation in which Jews were threatened with assimilation, and there were many outside Palestine who had already lost any living contact with their Hebrew roots. Even at Jerusalem, there were plenty of collaborators, who were prepared to adopt Roman laws and Greek ideas, and adapt their native Judaism to fit them. The Sadducees, for example, may have belonged to this group, and there were plenty of people who were prepared to offer their services to the foreign regime. Jesus came up against this when he was asked whether it was legitimate to pay taxes to Caesar, and the eruption of the Jewish revolt in AD 66 reminds us of what a powderkeg Palestine must have been at this time.

The desert was populated with different people and groups who offered resistance to the Romans and their influence, and the discovery of the Dead Sea scrolls in 1947 has revealed a good deal of their mentality to us. Like John, they were concerned for righteousness, and looked for an apocalyptic fulfilment of God's purposes. There were even some individuals who went around claiming to be the long-awaited Messiah. So who was to know whether there was anything special about John? By going to him for baptism, Jesus was affirming his ministry, and his claim to be the new Elijah whose coming had been prophesied by Malachi (Mal. 4:5). John understood that once Jesus came, his own ministry was virtually over, and we know that many of those who followed the Baptist later transferred their allegiance to Jesus. This is what John had intended, and by baptising Jesus in the way that he did, John bore witness to the ultimate purpose for which he had been sent.

The second main purpose of Jesus' baptism was to reveal the true nature of God's purposes. It was no accident that John called him 'the Lamb of God'. The lamb was the sacrificial animal used by the priests to make atonement every year in the temple. The idea that God would one day provide a sinless human being to be the great and final Lamb can be found in the Old Testament, especially in the curious incident recorded for us in Genesis 22, where Abraham was told to take his son Isaac up the mountain and sacrifice him. At the last minute, God told Abraham to desist, because he himself would provide a sacrifice, which for the time being was a ram which had got its horns caught in a nearby thicket. Obviously a ram was no real substitute for a human being, and we are left to conclude that if Abraham was expected to sacrifice his son and heir, then God would hardly do less. Nevertheless, this is a view from hindsight, and in John's day it remained hidden from most people's eyes. They were expecting quite a different kind of Messiah – a king in the tradition of David, who would rally the nation, chase away the Romans and restore the glory which had been promised to Israel a thousand years before, but which had been lost in the intervening centuries.

Jesus had to confront this misunderstanding throughout his career, even after his resurrection (Acts 1:6), and so we can see how deep-seated it must have been. But the crown which Jesus was called to wear was a crown of thorns, his throne would be the cross of Calvary, and his kingdom would be the society of believers who were prepared to forsake everything and follow him in expectation of their heavenly reward. This was not at all what the Jews had in mind, but however deep their misunderstanding may have been, the ministry of Jesus was set on its course right from the start. By accepting baptism, Jesus identified himself publicly with the sacrificial image of the Saviour, which subsequently became one of the basic themes of his preaching and teaching ministry. His death was not the unfortunate result of a failed rebellion, but the ultimate fulfilment of his saving purpose, and his baptism launched him on that very course.

The third purpose of Jesus' baptism was to reveal his relationship with God. Paul of Samosata believed that it was at this point that Jesus was adopted as the Son, but in fact Jesus' baptism was a public revelation of something which had been true all along. Once again, there was no secret about it – Jesus' public witness began with a clear affirmation of his divinity. Quite apart from the divine voice which sounded from heaven that Jesus was God's beloved Son, there was also the dove which settled on him. The dove is the symbol of the Holy Spirit, who appears for the first time at Jesus' baptism. There have been people of an adoptionist tendency who have viewed this as a kind of anointing by the Spirit, similar to what happens in Christian baptism. But a careful reading of the text will soon show that this view is untenable. The dove is not an integral part of the baptismal ceremony, but a witness to its significance. By appearing along with the Father's voice, the dove testifies to the Trinitarian reality of God, to which the Son belongs. He cannot be revealed in the fulness of his glory without the simultaneous revelation of the other persons of the Godhead. This is why he appears in Jesus' baptism, which is an assertion of Christ's divinity, not a concession to the weakness of his humanity.

Another aspect of Jesus' baptism which is easily overlooked is that it reminds us of the universal character of his mission. We have already stated that in Jewish circles, baptism was normally reserved for Gentile converts, and it seems more than likely that this aspect of Jesus' ministry was also in view at the time of his baptism. It is true, of course, that Jesus did not preach to Gentiles, and that he told even the Samaritans that salvation was of the Jews (John 4:22). The Gentile mission belongs to the post-Pentecostal period, in line with what Jesus said to his disciples shortly before his ascension into Heaven (Matt. 28:19). Nevertheless, we must not forget that John the Baptist hailed him as the Lamb of God who takes away the sins of the *world*, an expression which goes right against the normal Jewish exclusivity. At his baptism, Jesus was not looking forward only to his earthly mission, but also to the long-term fulfilment of his commission from the Father. It may in fact be this which lies behind Jesus' remark to John that his baptism was necessary in order to fulfil all righteousness (Matt. 3:15), since the ceremony had no place in the Jewish law.

Another aspect of Jesus' baptism which is implied more than it is clearly stated is that it was intended as a sign that he had come to claim his inheritance as the direct descendant of all those who had gone before him, to whom the promises of God had been given. This is apparent from Luke's Gospel, where the genealogy of Jesus is given immediately after the account of his baptism, and not (as in Matthew) in connection with his birth. A great deal has been written about these genealogies, which are very different both in form and content. Harmonizing them is not easy, but here we have to be very careful, because the Jews of Jesus' day had a very different attitude towards their ancestry than we have now. Most of us cannot think back more than three or four generations, but the Jews were much more inclined to keep a record of such things than we are. And of course, they were well aware of the ways in which genealogies could be used to prove whatever point they wanted to.

Some understanding of this can be gleaned from the one genealogy with which most of us are at least vaguely familiar – that of our own royal family. We all know that the throne is inherited, but the further back we go in time the more complex this is liable to get. Queen Elizabeth II is a direct descendant of Queen Victoria, and her lawful successor, but while she is also the lawful successor of Queen Elizabeth I, she is not a direct descendant of hers. It may come as a surprise to some people, but our present queen is a descendant of Mary, Queen of Scots, who was executed for taking part in a plot to put her on the English throne, but not of the legitimate sovereign whom Mary would have replaced. At the same time, the queen's entitlement to the throne owes as much to the fact that she is Elizabeth I's lawful successor as it does to the fact that she is Mary's physical descendant.

Complicated? Yes, indeed, but it should serve as a warning to us when we start to look at the Gospel genealogies. Apparent discrepancies may well turn out to be nothing of the kind if once we can recover the key to their interpretation. As long as we are not sure what the principles were on which the genealogies were constructed, we are unable to comment on apparent discrepancies between them. Looking at Luke's genealogy (which is the less familiar of the two), what we can say is that it is odd in at least two respects. First, it is a backward-looking genealogy, when most of the others we come across start with the remote ancestor and work down to the present. The description of someone as the 'son of' someone else does not normally stretch back beyond a generation or two at the most, but in this case, it goes back through no fewer than seventy-six generations! The second oddity is that the genealogy ends, not with Abraham or even with Adam, but with God, something which is quite unique. It is this second feature which helps us to understand Luke's purpose, because as far as he was concerned, the baptism of Jesus was part of his legitimation as Son of God. Luke is reminding us that this claim can be substantiated in human terms, as well as in divine ones. Of course, in purely human terms, we are all descended from Adam and so we could all presumably make the same claim, but as Luke traces the line of descent it becomes clear that Jesus' inheritance has passed down through a very special line, which includes the patriarchs to whom the promises were originally made, and the great King David, in whom they were confirmed.

But the line from David onwards is not at all what we would expect. There is not a single king of Israel or Judah mentioned in the list, not even Solomon! Jesus' claim to descent from David does not pass through that line, even if it is true that his claim to the royal succession must do. Evidently the direct royal line had died out, and it was only by collateral descent that Jesus was related to them. Again, our own royal family provides a parallel to this. The only Tudor ruler who is an ancestor of our queen is Henry VII, the founder of the dynasty. Likewise, she is descended from James VI (I) through his daughter Elizabeth, not though his son Charles I or either of his sons, even through they were all kings in their turn. Jesus could claim the inheritance of David without the embarrassment of having to acknowledge the paternity of any of his unworthy successors. It was at Jesus' baptism that the significance of this became apparent, because Jesus was not to be an earthly king in the line of David, but a spiritual ruler, keeping covenant with those who had gone before. This was to be the key to his ministry, through which he would be the spiritual heir to a kingdom not of this world. It is to the working out of that calling that we now turn.

5

The Temptations of Jesus
(Matthew 4:1-11)

If the baptism of Jesus was a revelation of his divinity, the temptations which followed immediately on it could hardly be a clearer reminder of his humanity. Of course, the way in which he resisted the temptations also bears witness to his divinity, but the event itself is something which only makes sense in a human context, because God cannot be tempted. There is at least one famous instance, in the first chapter of the book of Job, where Satan enters into dialogue with God on the subject of temptation and sin, but even there there is no suggestion that Satan was trying to lead God into sin. All he wanted was God's permission to let him have a go at Job, which was quite a different matter. Satan lacks the power to attack God in any way, but of course the concept of temptation has no meaning in the divine context. If God had yielded to a suggestion of Satan's it would not be yielding to temptation because it would not be a sin. Whatever God does is by definition without sin, whether Satan happens to agree with it or not. The fact that Jesus could be tempted is therefore a sign that he is truly human, and it is as a human being that he had to face the devil.

There has always been a strain in orthodox Christianity

which has found this hard to accept. Even though the Gospels tell us that Jesus was homeless, that he associated with the wrong kind of people and that he flouted the customs of polite Jewish society, most ordinary believers seem to want to make him as respectable as possible. In the Western world it often seems that the Church is irredeemably middle class, with all the expectations and prejudices which that implies. Jesus wore sandals and had a beard, but a minister who did the same today would meet with at least some opposition from parishioners who would feel that he was letting the side down. And no sensible clergyman today would spend time with publicans and prostitutes, whatever Jesus may have done. Jesus is held up as the model of the respectable citizen, however incongruous that may be, and whatever does not fit the image is simply glossed over and forgotten. He is portrayed as the perfect child, even though he abandoned his parents at the age of twelve and showed little remorse when they finally found him. He is held up as the ideal family man, even though he never married and told people that they could not be his disciples unless they were prepared to leave their families and follow him. And so on.

Occasionally people come along who sense this incongruity and protest against it. One of the more famous examples in modern times was the Greek writer Nikos Kazantzakis, who was so disturbed by what he saw as the Church's distortion of the Gospel message that he wrote a novel about it, *The Last Temptation of Christ*. For that, he was excommunicated by the Greek Church, but the novel made little impression elsewhere until it was made into a film. As soon as that happened, Christians who had never read the book or even heard of Kazantzakis could be found picketing cinemas where it was to be shown, on the ground that it was 'blasphemous'. It was certainly not a very good film, and it could be argued that the novel is not all that great either, but Kazantzakis' motive at least needs to be understood. He was protesting against a Jesus who had been made inhuman by an excess of pious devotion. The true Saviour was a flesh and blood man like the rest of us, exposed to the same temptations as we are, and susceptible to the same failures. If this were not the case, he would not have been one of us, and his saving work would have had no real meaning. Admittedly, Kazantzakis went too far in the other direction, but we ought to recognise at least that he was trying to put right an imbalance which he believed was harming the Church's witness to the world.

If Jesus was God in human flesh, were his temptations genuine? This question has often been asked, and answered in different ways. Long ago, it appears that Didymus the Blind of Alexandria (d. 398) believed that the temptations were not real, because Jesus, being God, could not have given in to them. This is an attractive, perhaps even a tempting (!) answer to this question, but it does not do proper justice to Christ's humanity. If Jesus had no real choice, then of course he was not really tempted, but if he was not really tempted, then he was not really human. It is perfectly true that we cannot imagine what would have happened if Jesus had given way to the devil, but however problematic that may be, it is the conclusion which is imposed on us by the two natures of Christ. He could have said yes to Satan, but he did not. This is not because he was God, because the Bible tells us that there is no temptation which has overtaken us which is too great for us to resist (1 Cor. 10:13).

So in what way can we say that Jesus' divinity is revealed in the temptations? The answer to this does not lie in his reaction to them, but in the nature of the temptations themselves. The writer to the Hebrews tells us that Jesus was tempted in every way, just as we are, yet without sin (Heb. 4:15), but the Bible never dwells on these. Sometimes Christians wonder whether Jesus was sexually tempted, and the answer has to be that he was, but no instance of this is recorded in the Gospels and we cannot read it into incidents such as his conversation with the woman at the well or his relations with Mary Magdalene. The New Testament is content to affirm the universal nature of Jesus' temptations without going into them in detail. What it does concentrate on though are the temptations which are not common to man – the temptations which were peculiarly his, because he was the Son of God.

This may seem strange at first sight, but we must remember that *all* temptation is geared to the individual being tempted. My weaknesses are not yours, and what tempts me may not bother you in the slightest. This is true even in the sexual realm. All of us are tempted to varying degrees in this realm, but even so we are tempted differently. If the Bible told us about Jesus' special temptations in this area, most people would find it more difficult, not less difficult to relate to him, because they would not be attracted by exactly the same things. We cannot share directly in Jesus' temptations, but at least we can recognise that they were peculiarly appropriate to him. I would not be tempted to turn stones into bread for the simple reason that I do not have the power to do so. I might be able to fantasise along those lines, but that is not the same thing at all. What made this a real temptation for Jesus was precisely the fact that he could do what the devil wanted – that is why it was a genuine temptation.

Once we accept that basic difference between him and us, we can begin to appreciate what the similarities are. First of all, the temptation was reasonable. Jesus was starving after having fasted for so long in the desert. Presumably there was no food shop in the neighbourhood, nor did he have any money to buy bread even if it had been available. But he had to eat sooner or later, so what could be more sensible than to use his power just for the sake of survival. You and I may live on a different level, but we can easily be tempted in the same kind of way. If we have special privileges or opportunities we may be tempted to use them to our own advantage, and many laws exist which try to limit this natural human tendency. But how many of us could honestly say that we would not take advantage of the contacts we have, especially if we thought that our life somehow depended on it? Furthermore, how many of us would believe that it was wrong to do something which was so obviously reasonable, and harmless to boot? Turning stones into bread was a good thing in itself, and this is the subtlest temptation of all. We can so easily find ourselves in situations where we can justify wrong behaviour in the name of a higher good, and the temptation to do so can be overwhelming at times. This is the situation which Jesus found himself in, but which he knew he had to resist. Why?

Jesus could not surrender to the devil's suggestion, not because it was harmful in itself, but because it went against the will of God. Part of Jesus' mission, and one of the main reasons why he went into the desert in the first place, was to demonstrate that man does not live by bread alone (Deut. 8:3). The truly spiritually-minded person will not be distracted by material concerns. He will know from his own experience that the lusts of the flesh, however understandable they may be, have a way of dulling the appetites of the spirit. People and nations which wallow in affluence are seldom as attentive to the things of God as they should be, while some of the most deeply spiritual people are those who have little or nothing of the goods of this world. In the rich countries of the West, the Church struggles to attract attention, whilst in the Third World it continues to spread like wildfire. Does this not tell us something about the way the devil can attack God's people – by making them rich? Jesus knew what the issue was, and he dealt with it in the same way that he expects us to deal with it – by saying no to the temptations of this world, and by turning away from its lures to the less obvious but infinitely deeper satisfactions offered by the Word of God.

Having got past that one, Jesus was next taken to the top of the temple in Jerusalem and asked to demonstrate his divinity by jumping off. Every once in a while there are people who commit suicide by jumping off some tall building or bridge, and so the nature of the devil's temptation is obvious. If Jesus could jump and live he would demonstrate that he could do the impossible, and people would follow him as a result. Jesus obviously wanted followers, and what better way could there be than to do something which would obviously attract the crowds? It is all very well to say that quality matters more than quantity, but very few people believe that in practice.

We live in a world which operates on the principle that the majority is right, and this attitude has affected the Church in many ways, not all of them subtle. We are familiar with the movement for 'church growth' as if this is a good in itself, and fail to notice that after a generation of mass evangelism, much of it geared to the lowest common denominator, Christian influence is weaker than it has ever been before. Jesus knew that he was better off with twelve men whom he could teach in depth than with thousands who merely turned up for miracles, and he acted accordingly. It is a lesson which we all need to learn, particularly when we have to evaluate the long-term effectiveness of our own ministries. Are we tempted to lean towards the spectacular in the hope of attracting crowds, even when in our hearts we know that this is not honouring to God? Resisting this kind of temptation is not easy, and many of us can testify with Jesus to the attractions of the easy answer.

Another important aspect of Christ's second temptation is the fact that the devil quoted Scripture in his attempt to persuade him. In this case it was Psalm 91:11-12, where God promised his people that he would protect them and lift them up in times of trouble, so that they would not 'strike their foot against a stone'. Naturally Satan quoted the verses out of context, and Jesus was not slow to point that out. God's promise was intended to reassure those who were in trouble, not to encourage reckless behaviour on the part of people who had no real problems but who merely wanted to show off. In the particular example given here, it may be said that if Jesus had been pushed off the roof of the temple against his will, God would have rescued him, but if he had jumped merely to show his power he might have come to a bad end instead.

It is extremely easy to focus on one particular biblical text, and rely on it to the exclusion of everything else. Scholars often stress the need to read each text within its wider context, but they have only a limited success in the churches. Part of the reason for this is that many Christians have been taught to relate the Bible to their own experience, and it can be all too easy to twist the meaning of text in order to make it fit what we want to believe. Unfortunately, scholars too are not immune to this. In the 1930s there were a number of German professors who suddenly discovered that the Bible was anti-Semitic, even though its context went completely against this. More recently, a number of theologians have discovered that the Bible supports such things as the ordination of women, or equal rights for homosexuals, even though nobody ever seems to have noticed this in the past.

Jesus dealt with this problem in the best way possible. Rather than argue at great length, he simply referred Satan to another biblical text which effectively killed his argument dead. This was Deuteronomy 6:16, which says: 'Do not put the Lord your God to the test.' Here is a general principle which can be applied in almost any circumstance, including the one which faced Jesus. It met the need of the moment, which was to tell the devil that he was off-base, but it also provided believers with a solid base for their own behaviour in any situation. We are not to presume on our relationship with God by daring him to demonstrate his power, whether it is necessary or not. If we put ourselves in a position which we should never have found ourselves in in the first place, we cannot blame God if he does not come to our rescue. No sensible person would play with fire or with electricity just to show what these things can do. But if we are wise with the powers of this world, how much more should we be careful to watch what we do with the far greater power of God. He will not be mocked by our foolishness, and if we do not realise that, then the likelihood is that we shall lose out in the end.

The last temptation was the most serious of all. Satan, who is the prince of this world, offered to turn his power over to Jesus, if only the latter would bow down and worship him. Selling one's soul to the devil may seem like a rather dramatic and extravagant thing to do, and most of us probably feel that it is something very far removed from anything we are likely to contemplate. But we need to remember that it is remarkably similar to the temptation which Satan gave to Adam and Eve. They did not fall because they rebelled against God, but because they tried to become more like him. Satan told them that all they had to do was to eat of the fruit of the tree of the knowledge of good and evil, and presto – they would be just like God! What Adam and Eve did in effect was to sell themselves to Satan, with the result that he became the prince of this world and has exercised his control over us ever since. The only reason that the temptation offered to Jesus may seem odd to us is that we have already fallen into it.

The main difference between us and Jesus at this point is that he could see clearly what the issue was, and because he was sinless, he had the perspective needed to avoid falling into the trap set for Adam and Eve. We, on the other hand, who were born in a state of sin and rebellion against God, are just not able to make such decisions. The temptation means nothing to us because we have already surrendered to it.

This changes only when we are born again and enter into a living relationship with God in Christ. When that happens, we are delivered from our spiritual blindness and given the power to see evil for what it is. Indeed, spiritual warfare and the great struggle against the rule of Satan are only meaningful to Christians, because only they have been enlightened and made sensitive to the issues involved. It is not a comfortable position to be in, but it is far better than the alternative, which is to be under

Satan's thumb. The Christian life is not easy, but it is infinitely better than what we have been delivered from.

Jesus responds to Satan in the best way he can, by quoting a version of the first commandment (Deut. 6:13). We are commanded to worship only the Lord our God, and to obey him in everything we do. Obedience is the key to the Christian life, the true test of our relationship with God. Jesus said to his disciples that he called them friends, but then added that they were his friends only if they did whatever he commanded them (John 15:14). This is not the normal human pattern, where such a relationship would be seen as one of domination, and thus the very opposite of true friendship. But in our life with God, we must respect him for who he is – our creator and Lord. In that context, obedience is the natural thing, and without it, we cannot live in his presence. Jesus laid it on the line very clearly, and we must do the same when the devil comes to tempt us away from our salvation.

God will not let us down if we commit ourselves fully to him. When Jesus resisted, the devil went away, and in his place, God sent angels to minister to Jesus' needs. If we stand up to the temptations which come our way we shall find exactly the same thing in our own experience. We never sacrifice anything for God's sake which is not given back to us a hundred times over. Jesus got his kingdom in the end, and it is a kingdom which far outshines the splendour of the lands which the devil offered him. Having passed the test, he was ready for his triumph, and the devil never again got a foothold in his life, even when he was suffering and dying on the cross.

May God grant us the grace to face the tests when they come, and to win through them to the glory which awaits us around the throne of God.

6

The Transfiguration
(Matthew 17:1-9; Mark 9:2-10; Luke 9:28-36)

One of the most famous but least understood stories of the life of Jesus is the account of his transfiguration 'on a high mountain' (traditionally thought to have been Mt. Tabor) shortly before his passion. The story has frequently been at the centre of mystical experiences of various kinds, and it was a major element in the spiritual exaltation of the so-called 'Taborites' in fifteenth-century Bohemia. They were people who took the teaching of Jan Hus and combined it with an extreme form of millennarianism which was eventually crushed by the authorities. Among the eastern Orthodox it has always been a major feast, celebrated in religious folklore as much as in the Church's liturgy. Nearer to home, although the Transfiguration appears as a minor feast in the calendar of the Book of Common Prayer (6 August), it has never played a very important part in the life of the Church and the event has been largely ignored in popular spirituality and devotion.

The sheer strangeness of the transfiguration, and perhaps also its association with mysticism, has helped to push it into the background of Church life as far as most of us are concerned. Who would preach on it, or venture to explain its deeper implications? The difficulty which it can cause is amply demonstrated by the belief, held by some German scholars, that it is really a post-resurrection narrative which somehow got displaced in the early tradition. A careful reading of the text will show the implausibility of this thesis, which has never received widespread support, but the fact that it has been seriously suggested indicates just how difficult it is to know what to make of the transfiguration.

This is a great pity, because the Gospel accounts of the transfiguration are among the most important sources for our Christology. The transfiguration offers a glimpse into the self-understanding of Jesus which reveals the hidden depths of his being and explains the purpose of his coming in a way which is unique in the Gospels. Because of this, if we fail to understand it we are in danger of failing to understand Christ.

The first point to be made about it is that the transfiguration is a revelation of God in Jesus Christ. Here we must pay the closest attention to the word used to describe the event. The Greek term is *metamorphosis*, which means a change of *morphe*, or form. In Greek thought, the form is the appearance or shape of an object. Together with substance, it is a constituent part of every being. The precise relationship between these two was (and to some extent still is) hotly debated. Most people believed that it was possible to change the form of a thing without changing its substance. In other words, bread could be in the form of loaves or rolls yet still be considered the same substance. Some, however, have maintained that form and substance are inextricably linked.

Change one and you will change the other. This view has been held in our own day by Marshall Mcluhan, whose famous dictum 'the medium is the message' sums it up nicely. Finally, Roman Catholics have maintained that it is possible to alter the substance without changing the form. Thus they claim that a wafer can become the body of Christ without losing the form of bread. Unfortunately these philosophical distinctions have been lost in popular speech, with the result that the English word *transformation* now tends to imply a change of substance as well as form. A butterfly is more than a transformed caterpillar, but it would be misleading to say that the caterpillar had been transubstantiated.

The distinction is an important one however, and has been carefully guarded by using the word *transfiguration*. Jesus underwent a change of form designed to reveal the underlying substance – his divinity. Even more important, this change did not involve the removal of his human nature, as if it were a mask concealing an incomprehensible divinity. The transfiguration confirmed the integrity of Jesus' humanity and the appropriateness of using it as the means of expressing his divine presence in the world.

In an age in which it is widely believed that God and man are 'wholly other' – incompatible by nature and therefore incapable of entering into a meaningful personal relationship – reaffirming the transfiguration is a matter of supreme importance. Human nature has a place in God's plan, and is not alien to his being. On the mount Jesus revealed to his disciples how divinity and humanity could co-exist in a single person, and in doing so he gave us some indication of what our own resurrection bodies will be like.

At the same time, however, Jesus also revealed that his incarnation was an end in itself. It has always been a temptation to interpret the image of the Church as the body of Christ in terms which make it an extension of the incarnation, as if the latter were somehow incomplete, or had some purpose to fulfil which went beyond the earthly work of Christ. This is particularly true of Roman Catholicism, which goes so far as to call Mary the mother of the Church, because she was the vehicle of the incarnation. But it can be found in Evangelical circles too, especially among those who regard social concern and political involvement as a major part of the gospel. These people may be tempted to justify caring for 'the whole man' theologically by referring to the incarnation as the model for Christian living. The incarnation can even be used to argue that physical healing is an integral part of salvation to which believers are automatically entitled.

The transfiguration serves as a corrective to these ideas by putting them in their proper context. The redemption of humanity is not ruled out – on the contrary! – but it is put within the proper framework. In this world, the Church receives no more than a glimpse of the glory which is to be revealed to us at the end of time. Jesus was not transfigured in order to fulfil his mission then and there, but in order to give the disciples a picture of the life to come. Like them, we catch only glimpses of the resurrection glory, which are a foretaste of our inheritance in Heaven. Peter understood this in later life, and wrote as much to the early Church (2 Pet. 1:16-18). The Christian life, as we know it now, is a wonderful thing in many ways, but what awaits us in glory is infinitely greater and more wonderful. Christians are pilgrims on earth, heading for Heaven, and whatever blessings we may enjoy here and now, they are no substitute for what is to come in eternity.

Another important aspect of the transfiguration is that it sets Jesus within the context of Old Testament Judaism. When Peter saw Moses and Elijah with Jesus, he suggested that three tabernacles be built to honour each of the men. The implications of this are clear enough. Jesus was to be given a certain priority, by being placed first, possibly out of deference, but essentially he would be the equal of the great prophets of Israel. In reality though, the appearance of the two patriarchs demonstrates not Jesus' equality with them but his superiority to them.

First, it is to be noted that Jesus appeared alone to begin with. His clothing is described as dazzling white, the colour which represents the pure light of God. Moses and Elijah appeared subsequently, and they were visible only in the light of Jesus and in relation to him. Jesus could converse with them as well as with the disciples, but the disciples could speak only to Jesus, who is thus revealed as the link between the living and the departed. Moses and Elijah represent the Law and the Prophets, the two strands of Old Testament teaching to which Jesus appealed as witnesses of his coming. Both bear witness to him and both are *glorified*, i.e. revealed in their spiritual nature, in the light of Christ – and only in that light.

The transfiguration is therefore of the greatest importance for what it teaches about the fulfilment of the Old Testament in Christ. We are reminded of Moses' transfiguration at Sinai, when he had to veil himself in front of the people. Paul used that incident in order to describe the blindness of the Jews, and it is entirely possible that the transfiguration is also harking back to Sinai and the inability of Israel to tolerate the full ray of divine light, even as it was reflected in the face of Moses. The disciples, however, had been exposed to the full brightness, and had not been blinded by it.

The experience of the mountaintop is also of great importance for what it teaches about *the spiritual life* of Christ's followers. Notice that the disciples were sleepy, a detail which is reminiscent of Gethsemane. For some reason it seems that the most spiritually intense moments in the earthly life of Jesus were accompanied by a noticeable drowsiness in the disciples. Just when they should have been awake with excitement, they are portrayed as distracted and uninterested. Why?

The answer, it would appear, is that this corresponds to a peculiar experience of all believers. Whether we are mystics speaking of *acedia*, that listlessness which comes to dampen the intensity of the spiritual life, or whether we are sober-minded, no-nonsense Evangelicals talking about dryness and a certain tiredness of the soul, the effect is the same. We find that, in our walk with God, the weakness of the flesh intervenes to prevent us from watching and waiting on the Lord in the way we know we should. Many good Christians suffer untold agonies because they feel unable to confess to such an 'unspiritual' failure, and great discouragement can result. But this experience is common to the saints, and is shown in Scripture to be the prelude to great things in the presence of God.

This does not mean that the Bible approves of such lassitude, or encourages it in us as a means of spiritual growth. If mechanical exercises cannot bring us nearer to God, how can we expect deliberate indifference to do so? The point is not that laziness is a virtue, but that the flesh is weak and not to be trusted. What spiritual pride might have resulted, if the disciples had been able to think that the transfiguration was the reward for their watchfulness. But the New Testament constantly reminds us that it is when we are least expecting it that God enters our lives, bringing both judgement on our failure to serve him as we ought, and a redemption which we have done nothing to deserve.

However, the thorniest question connected with the disciples is not this, but the problem of *mystical* experience. At various times in the history of the Church people have claimed that they too have been transfigured in the uncreated light of Mt. Tabor. In some contemplative traditions of monasticism it has become the cherished goal to which the Christian should aim by means of spiritual exercises and ascetic discipline. Is there anything in the text which could support these claims or encourage such behaviour?

When considering the mystical aspect of the transfiguration, it is important to remember the difference between Moses and Elijah on the one hand, and the disciples on the other. Both stand in relationship to Jesus, but the former represent the Church triumphant whilst the latter are as yet 'the Church militant here on earth'. Far from being trivial, this distinction is of the utmost importance. The disciples witnessed the transfiguration of others in an event which was primarily intended to be a revelation of the heavenly glory. They did *not* participate in this transfiguration themselves, nor did they experience a foretaste of the glory which would one day be revealed in them. This revelation of glory in us, which the whole creation awaits with eager anticipation, is not a flash of lightning erupting into the world as an ecstatic experience, but a permanent reality which will be established at the end of time (Rom. 8:18-19).

Having said that, it remains true that the disciples did enter into the mystery of the transfiguration in a way which goes beyond rational explanation. We must never let a false interpretation of spiritual experience influence us to the point where we discount such things altogether. Luke 9:34 tells us plainly that a cloud came and enveloped the disciples when they were gazing at the three men transfigured. In many parts of Scripture the cloud is the symbol of the presence of God, but it also reminds us of the distance which still remains between us and the heavenly glory. In terms of visual understanding, it is truly the 'cloud of unknowing', a reminder that we walk by faith, not by sight.

At the same time, however, this unknowing is not to be equated with ignorance, or with separation from God. On the contrary, it is in the cloud that God speaks to the disciples and bears witness to his Son Jesus. It was not the vision by itself which told them this, since Peter imagined Jesus to be more or less on a par with Moses and Elijah. A clear explanation of who Jesus was came only when the vision itself was obscured.

This point is of great importance because it testifies to the nature of Christian experience. Many people feel that there would be some advantage in seeing Jesus face to face, that 'seeing is believing'. Yet whilst the Bible does not discount the value of the disciples' experience, it quite clearly puts the emphasis on the fact that they encountered God by *hearing his voice*. The priority of hearing over seeing is a constant factor in the whole of the biblical revelation. It is no accident that when Peter referred to this incident, he did so in the context of exalting the Scriptures as the recorded speech of God. The Church militant sees through a glass darkly and not face to face (1 Cor. 13:12) but we have the words of God to bear witness to the glory which will be revealed in and to us.

Lastly we must consider briefly the temptation which Peter had, to record the experience of the transfiguration in monuments of brick and mortar. Christians are often inclined to hark back to the great moments of the past, especially the experience of conversion, and set these up in their minds as the norm for the Christian life. Jesus does not attack this desire, but neither does he respond to it directly. For him, each spiritual experience is a signpost on the journey, an encouragement to go on to greater things. The Christian life must never get stuck in the past, but must press on to further heights. The disciples were told not to broadcast what had happened, but to wait until after the resurrection, when the meaning of their experience would become clear.

There may have been many motives for this command of Jesus, but it is interesting to note what is recorded in Scripture. According to Mark 9:10 they kept the matter to themselves, discussing what 'rising from the dead' might mean. In other words, at the very moment of greatest exaltation, when the temptation to spiritual pride must have been strongest, Jesus challenged them with a whole new idea. Here was something they had not yet witnessed, a further step which they would have to take before they could speak about what had just happened. The transfiguration was not an end in itself but a stage on the journey into Christ, the Son of Man and the Son of God. As Christians, we must grasp the teaching contained in this great event and apply it to ourselves so that when he comes again we too may enter into his transfiguration glory and bear witness with Moses, Elijah and all the company of Heaven that Jesus Christ is indeed King of Kings and Lord of Lords, to the glory of God the Father.

7

The Crucifixion
(Matthew 27:32-56; Mark 15:21-41;
Luke 23:26-49; John 19:16-37)

The story of the crucifixion is easily the best known and most frequently remembered event recorded in the New Testament. Even the nativity stories, despite their familiarity, tend to be trotted out only once a year. But the death of Jesus, quite apart from the special significance attached to Good Friday, is recalled to our minds by every cross we see, by every Communion service we attend, by a large number of evangelistic sermons and books, and by the personal testimony of all who have found peace with God through the shed blood of Christ. Other things can be put aside or neglected for a time, but there is no getting away from the cross, which stands at the heart of Christianity.

The central place which the cross occupies in the Christian life is no accident, and believers are usually prompt to point out its significance. It was on the cross that the Son of God became sin for us, paying the debt we owe to God, satisfying the demands of his law and justice, making atonement for man's disobedience, and bringing reconciliation to those who were dead in trespasses and sins, giving us an entry by his sacrifice into the holy of holies, into the presence of God himself. This interpretation, which is technically known as the 'penal substitutionary theory' of the atonement, has met with considerable opposition from those who find such an idea immoral or barbaric, but we must not be deterred by this. Experience has shown that it alone holds the key to the mystery of Christ's death, and has the power to change men's lives. When the apostle Paul went to Corinth, he knew what the objections would be, but this did not prevent him from saying that he was determined to know nothing among the Corinthians but Christ, and Christ crucified (1 Cor. 2:2).

Paul's reasons for saying this are clear enough. As an apostle, his business was to preach the wisdom and the power of God, not to pander to the logic or the convenience of men. It is a point which can easily be forgotten, especially by preachers who feel compelled to preach on politics, social welfare, family life and other more 'relevant' topics. The message of Scripture on this score is plain enough – for the Christian, 'relevance' is to be found only in the cross, which is God's saving message 'to all who are called'. The Church is not a social service agency, nor is it a body of well-intentioned people seeking to do good. It is a motley collection of the weak, the foolish, the despised and the rejected – men and women whom the world does not want, but who have found their peace and their glory in the calling of Jesus Christ.

Today we are in desperate need of a renewed emphasis on the atonement, both in our preaching and in our spiritual life. It may be that some ears have grown dull with hearing, though experience suggests that such ears are just as likely to belong to the preacher as to members of the congregation. Sin is not a popular subject in today's 'adult' climate. These days we are asked to accept everything and to expect little or nothing from others. What was once perceived as failure and inadequacy is now explained as difference, which may be due to background, culture, education, personality or whatever, but cannot be attributed to wilful rebellion or disobedience, which is the traditional understanding of sin. In such a context, the notion of reconciliation has lost any meaning, because if we truly loved others we would try to understand them and avoid a falling-out in the first place. God's willingness to forgive us when we do not deserve it smacks of judgement, which is by definition unloving and repressive. Why does he not just accept us as we are and let us do as we like, so that we can fulfil our potential without the restraints imposed on us by standards which are probably no more than the prejudices of others?

The subtle transition from a gospel of forgiveness to a message of acceptance without qualification is a perversion of the Evangelical faith which has crept into more than one pulpit almost certainly unawares. Yet the atoning work of Christ on the cross does not mean, as the third eucharistic prayer in the Church of England's Alternative Service Book (1980) has it, that 'he opened wide his arms for us on the cross'. He did nothing of the kind. Jesus' arms were outstretched and nailed to the cross as a sign of his human impotence as the sacrificial victim, not as a sign of welcome to future Church members. Christ did not reach down from the cross to respond to the needs of the world; rather he looked up from the cross to his Father, whose will he was doing and whose wrath he was appeasing. The effect, of course, was to meet the world's need, but in a way which the world could not understand. What we now experience as God's free forgiveness comes with the greatest price tag in the world attached to it – the lifeblood of the Son of God. Access to its saving power is open to everyone who believes, but a vital part of this belief is the recognition that we are sinners in need of forgiveness, and not just lonely, isolated people who are looking for a hug from God.

The importance of this teaching on the atonement must always be safeguarded against attacks, especially when they come in such subtle ways as these. What a tragedy it would be if, after having defended the gospel against the assaults of late nineteenth and early twentieth century liberalism, we should now find ourselves succumbing to the lure of pop psychology. But unfortunately, there is every indication that most people no longer think of Christ as our heavenly judge, but rather as a kind of supernatural guidance counsellor – a shoulder to cry on rather than a hand to guide and direct us along the paths of righteousness.

Furthermore, we need to remember that although atonement might have been made in other ways, the crucifixion is given to us not merely as a picture to help us understand its cost, but also as a model to guide and direct our own spiritual life. Here there is a great mystery which needs to be carefully pondered. God knew that only he could provide the sacrifice which was needed to deal once and for all with the problem of sin. No human being could make atonement on his own behalf, or contribute in any way to his own salvation. God knew that the only way a sinful man could enter into his presence was by dying and rising again to a new life, one which was free from the bondage of sin. Death was the easy part, and because of sin, all men had to suffer it. But this death had no redeeming virtue, and was quite incapable of leading to new life. On the other hand, the Holy Trinity could not receive into their fellowship any sinner who had not undergone that process of transformation which only death and rebirth can provide.

The theological basis for this change is the death of Christ for us on the cross. He had no sin to atone for, and had no need to die for his own benefit. It is interesting to note here that Muslims, who deny the divinity of Christ, nevertheless accept that he was a man without sin, and therefore they deny that he was ever crucified at all. In Islamic belief, it was Judas who was put to death in the place of Jesus, who supposedly ascended straight to Heaven. We can appreciate Muslim scruples in this respect, but at the same time we have to recognise that they have completely missed the point. Jesus died in order to remove the barrier of death and give us new life in him. He could certainly have gone straight to Heaven, but if he had done so, we would not now be able to follow him there.

It is sometimes objected that even if Christ did die for our sins, we are still unworthy to stand in the presence of God. The Roman Catholic church has dealt with this problem by inventing the concept of purgatory, in which sinners can work off their sins after death, in preparation for eventual entry into Heaven. Protestants agree that there is a difficulty here, but they resolve it in a totally different way. John Wesley stated the Protestant position very clearly when he said that he took himself to Christ for sanctification as well as for justification. In Wesley's theology, 'took himself to Christ' can only mean that he relied entirely on Christ's atoning work on the cross. The New Testament teaches that the cross is *both* the unique atoning work of Jesus which justifies us in the sight of God *and* the basis on which that justification is applied to sanctify our lives. In the process of sanctification, the crucifixion of Christ becomes an experience which is shared by us, as we take up our cross and follow him. In this way the believer, who is justified by faith, is admitted to the privilege of sharing in the sufferings of Christ (cf. 2 Tim. 2:12), by which we are sanctified.

Paul makes this point on any number of occasions. Writing to the Galatians about justification, he says at the end that he bears in his body the marks of the Lord Jesus (Gal. 6:17). The possibility of a purely spiritual interpretation of this is excluded by what he says elsewhere, as for example in 2 Corinthians 4:10, where 'the dying of the Lord Jesus' is explicitly related to his own sufferings and persecutions. Paul did not suffer, as Christ did, exclusively on behalf of others, though some might interpret the text in this way, but also because there was a process of sanctification going on in his own life, which was necessary for his own spiritual growth as well as for the expansion of the Church. Paul did not claim some special relationship with Jesus on the ground that he was an apostle, but recognised that all believers are admitted to the fellowship of his sufferings (Phil. 3:10), a point which is made even more clearly by the apostle Peter (1 Pet. 4:13).

Furthermore, the biblical call to suffering and self-denial in the service of Christ is constantly related to the crucifixion. 'I am crucified with Christ, nevertheless I live' (Gal. 2:20), says Paul. He is not speaking here only of the fact that he has been justified, but also of the fact that he is currently being sanctified as well. The crucifixion is present at the heart of each stage of the Christian's pilgrimage, not just at the beginning.

There is obviously a great deal which can be said about the Christian's calling to mortify the flesh, but in view of the link we have established with the crucifixion, it seems best to look primarily at the words of Jesus on the cross which have special relevance to this theme. There are two of these, both of them recorded for us only in John's Gospel.

The first is found in John 19:26-27: 'Woman, behold thy son. Son, behold thy mother.' In these words we sense the *pain of renunciation* as Jesus tears himself away from his only blood relative on earth. Of course there are many hints of this renunciation throughout the Gospels. One might even say that the evangelists were at pains to distance Jesus from his human family – from his mother in particular. It comes out in the story when he was in the temple at the age of twelve, in the wedding feast at Cana and later on during his ministry (Matt. 12:48-50).

Yet in none of these instances can we really speak of a full renunciation. During his earthly ministry, Jesus never abandoned his family, although this idea formed part of his teaching (Mark 10:29). True renunciation came only as he was about to depart this life, and the poignancy of the experience is brought home only on the cross. For not only was Jesus giving up his mother, he was giving his own place in her affections to someone else. We are accustomed to look at this from a modern perspective, and imagine that Jesus was providing his mother with security in her old age, or something of the kind. This is not impossible, but Jesus had half-brothers who could have taken the responsibility without being asked, and the cross was hardly the place to make such a domestic arrangement!

In examining the meaning of this verse, the wider context of Jesus' suffering must be taken as the basic framework for our interpretation. It is *his* pain which we are discussing, not that of the onlookers. Seen in this light, a verse which otherwise is little more than a touching detail becomes a vital challenge to every believer. How many of us are prepared to put God before family? Of course, our families are a responsibility which we cannot neglect; Jesus did not abandon Mary, or leave her without support. But how many of us would be prepared to share our families as he did, to commit our loved ones to the care of others, even for a short time? Is our attachment to our human relations basically a selfish desire for love and affection which we are not prepared to extend to others? And are we so bound up with them that they come before God's call to us?

These questions need to be faced with great urgency today. Many Christians have responded to the pressures put on the nuclear family in modern society by trying to reinforce the blood-tie to the exclusion of everything else. Marriage enrichment courses, family development seminars and the like are becoming increasingly popular, even to the point where the impression is given that it is right and proper for a believer to seek fulfilment in these things as if they were an end in themselves. Yet how can what is transitory ever offer eternal satisfaction? The Bible tells us that the person who wants to save his life will lose it, whereas the one who loses his life for Christ's sake will be saved for evermore. The man or woman who puts parents, spouse or children before Christ is bound to lose them, because God has not been given first place. Are we producing a generation of Christians who will never be satisfied or content with what they have, because they have never learned the basic principles of self-denial?

The second word from the cross is 'I thirst' (John 19:28). Here again various interpretations have been suggested, but the 'naturalistic' ones (e.g. that vinegar would help soothe the pain and speed up death) are both trivial and excluded by the reference to Psalm 69:21, where no such idea is entertained. In Psalm 69 the writer is speaking of the depths of degradation to which his sufferings have driven him. Those on whom he might have leaned for support have turned against him, offering only vinegar and gall to meet his suffering. By identifying with this, Jesus points to yet another aspect of his suffering, *the bitterness of rejection*. It is a theme which occurs frequently in the Scriptures, from Isaiah 53:3 to John 1:11. Jesus himself rebuked the Jews for their refusal to accept him and his teaching, and we find a similar rejection in the ministry of Paul who was turned out of the synagogues and opposed even within some of the churches he had founded.

All this is familiar enough. What is perhaps less often realised is that both Jesus and Paul suffered pain in being rejected. The Son of God did not come to strangers. He came to his own, and it was they who refused to receive him. Again, we know that rejection formed part of the teaching of Jesus. He prophesied that his message would bring a sword which would divide families and friends (Matt. 10:34). Yet only on the cross did he himself experience that ultimate rejection of which he had spoken. His disciples deserted him. His nation acquiesced in his crucifixion, even to the point of begging the Roman authorities to put him to death in spite of Pilate's declaration of his innocence.

The way of the cross is the way of rejection by men. We are blessed when men revile us and persecute us, saying all kinds of false things against us for his sake (Matt. 5:11). Today churches bend over backwards to please, to attract the unbeliever, to demonstrate how Christians, too, are concerned with the issues which disturb the world.

When courageous people like Mary Whitehouse and Anne Atkins stand out against sin in society, it is all too often the church authorities who attack them, along with the secular media. The bitterness of rejection can often be felt most keenly within the visible household of faith. The agony of Christ may well be shared by his disciples in this respect as in others.

This being said, there is one danger which must be avoided. Jesus told his disciples that they must take up their cross in order to follow him (Matt. 16:24). What does this mean? Some have thought that a believer should seek out a cross, as a burden to be borne. Others have regarded every setback, misfortune or illness as a cross sent to them by God. Many have derived a perverse sense of satisfaction, even pride, from the pains they have endured supposedly for the cause of Christ. What should be said about this? First, taking up the cross is a *commitment*. When the sign of the cross is given in baptism, it is given as a reminder of the commitment expected of the newly baptised.

Second, to take up the cross is to prepare oneself for the suffering which will come as we *follow* him. The second part of Christ's command is indispensable, because it balances the first part. Suffering is never an end in itself. The crucifixion was grounded in obedience – not my will, but thy will be done – and consummated in the glory of the resurrection. The Christian believer must follow his Lord in this as in everything else. To exalt the one aspect out of its context is to court disaster. The crucifixion is central, but in the life of Jesus it lasted only three hours.

Obedience on the other hand is eternal, as is the resurrection glory, which will be revealed in us when the sufferings of the present time are over (Rom. 8:18).

8

The Resurrection
(Matthew 28; Mark 16; Luke 24; John 20-21)

'If Christ has not been raised, your faith is vain; you are still in your sins' (1 Cor. 15:17). Paul's warning reminder to the Corinthian Church is the natural place to begin any discussion of the resurrection, not least because it is in this same passage that he makes the link between Christ's resurrection and ours. Here, indeed, is something truly remarkable. We have not participated in his incarnation, in his transfiguration or in his atoning death, but we are told quite explicitly by the Apostle Paul that resurrection from the dead will be as much a part of our experience as it was of the experience of the human Jesus. Of course, Paul does not say that the details of our resurrection will parallel that of Christ's any more than our death is likely to be the same as his. Indeed, much of what he writes on the subject, both here and in 1 Thessalonians 4–5, may fairly be said to be an explanation of how our resurrection will *differ* from his. But however much the events may vary, the principle remains the same. Like Jesus, we shall overcome death, and we shall share with him in the eternal life of God.

The first point we must bear in mind when we consider this subject is the importance of the resurrection for *faith*.

We must not fall into the trap of thinking that coming back from the dead is enough by itself to produce belief in our hearts. Jesus criticised Thomas because he insisted on this kind of proof, but if that is what we want we shall certainly be disappointed. Faith does not come by witnessing miracles, however sensational they may be, but by hearing the Word of God. The disciples had a measure of faith even before Jesus' death (e.g. Matt. 16:16) and there were still questions in their minds after he rose from the dead (e.g. Acts 1:6-7). The resurrection does not create faith, and rejecting it does not necessarily destroy it. There are people today who profess faith in Christ, but who find the idea of a bodily resurrection incredible, but much as orthodox believers feel inclined to discount such professions, it is doubtful whether they are justified in doing so merely on the ground that belief in the resurrection is an essential part of their faith. What the Bible says is not that faith without the resurrection is impossible, but that it is vain – it is empty and devoid of content.

The reason why this is so is also clearly stated in the text. It is not primarily a question of death, though that certainly comes into it, but of *sin*. Without the resurrection we are still in our sins, which can only mean that the atoning work of Christ is not complete without the resurrection. Here we Protestants face a challenge to our traditional outlook. How often have we heard it said that Christ's words on the cross, *It is finished!*, indicate the completion of his atoning work, as if from that moment onward the whole work of reconciliation has been accomplished? How often have we concentrated so strongly on the *theologia crucis* that we have neglected the *theologia gloriae*, failing to perceive that these are two sides of the same coin? It is no disparagement of the crucifixion to say that even Christ's sacrifice would have been in vain had he not risen from the dead, had he not demonstrated that he has not merely paid the price for sin but has overcome its power as well. The resurrection is demonstrable proof that his sacrifice was acceptable to God the Father, and that we have been delivered from the bondage of death. The crucifixion deals with our past, by paying the price for our sins. The resurrection, on the other hand, looks to our future, when we shall dwell with Christ and reign with him in the heavenly places.

Of course, statements of this kind run the danger of appearing to deny the sufficiency of Christ's atoning work on the cross. This danger is real, and it must certainly be avoided if we are to present a true picture of Christ's redemption. But we must not stress the crucifixion to the point where the resurrection is allowed to fade into the background, as if it were a kind of anticlimax, or appendix to the main event. Christ's suffering and death were not ends in themselves; they led inevitably to victory over the power of sin and to a new life in the eternal love of God. The Christian message is not merely one of forgiveness of sin, however important that may be; it is also one of hope that out of death will come a new and better life. This emphasis must never be lost, even as we give the appropriate weight to other aspects of Christ's saving work. Without the resurrection our faith is vain because we have no hope left, nothing to point to as the fulfilment of our present life of trust and obedience.

The resurrection of Christ cancels out the power of sin and death in a way which nothing else ever could, and for this reason it rightly receives the highest place of honour in our worship and in our preaching. But in wiping out the effects of sin, the resurrection does not automatically take away all trace of suffering. Christ's body continues to bear the marks of his crucifixion, an important reminder of the ongoing validity of his atoning sacrifice. Scripture bears witness to this, because when Jesus appeared to Thomas, he asked him to touch his hands and side, where the marks of the wounds were still plainly visible. Late medieval piety had apparently developed the idea that the wounds were still open, so that they remain in eternity as fountains of Christ's blood, which is constantly pouring out to wash away the sins of men. It was against such a distortion that Calvin protested in his commentary of Luke 24:13-35. According to him, the wounds were no longer visible, because if they had been, the men on the road to Emmaus would have recognised Jesus straightaway.

It is always dangerous to argue from silence, and it would appear that, in this instance, Calvin's desire to avoid a particular abuse pushed him too far in the opposite direction. The marks of Christ's wounds have no saving significance in themselves, and they can certainly not add anything to what he accomplished on the cross but they are still important for what they tell us about the benefits of our salvation. The apostle Paul tells us that bearing in our bodies the marks of the Lord Jesus is part of our enjoyment of the firstfruits of the Kingdom (2 Cor. 4:10). Paul cannot possibly mean by this that we are helping to earn our own salvation, since that would contradict the whole tenor of his gospel message. What he means is that suffering is part of our *glory*, one of the privileges which comes from being in fellowship with Jesus. Today there is a strong temptation to preach a gospel of ease and comfort, in which the resurrection is seen as automatic deliverance from all pain. That may be true eschatologically, in the sense that when we rise from the dead our troubles will be over. It is most emphatically not true, however, of the relationship which we now enjoy with the risen Christ. There is a suffering which we still have to endure, so that the life of Christ might be spread abroad in the world. When he rose from the dead Christ did not destroy all memory of his suffering, but held it out as an example for us to follow in the work of spreading the gospel.

The resurrection of Jesus is portrayed in the New Testament as the beginning of an interim period which culminated in his ascension forty days later. The symbolism implicit in the number 'forty' will not be lost on students of the Scriptures, who will remember that Jesus fasted for forty days in the wilderness, that the people of Israel spent forty years in the desert, and so on. Forty is the mark of completion, an indication that everything which can reasonably be expected has been accomplished. It was during this time that Jesus taught his disciples, by reminding them of what he had said before his crucifixion, and by drawing out the saving significance of the great events of his passion.

Let us consider for a moment what the significance of the forty days between Christ's resurrection and his ascension really was. First there is the fact of his *appearances* to his disciples. The Gospel records have sometimes been discounted on the grounds that he appeared only to believers, not to those outside his circle, though the case of Thomas ought to suggest that not all of Jesus' disciples were prepared to swallow such a tale without critical examination. Mary Magdalene may conceivably have been in a state of hysteria in the Garden, as Michael Goulder suggested in *The Myth of God Incarnate*, a notorious symposium which appeared in 1977, but even if she was, there is no indication that it was catching – especially not over a period of forty days! Had Jesus appeared only once to one person, or in exactly the same way to two or three people, there would also be considerable ground for suspicion. But the sheer variety of his post-resurrection appearances makes the idea of a collective hallucination exceedingly improbable, to say the least. It is also important to note the fine balance which is maintained in these appearances between the human and the divine. Jesus is capable of appearing and vanishing at will, which rules out any theory of resuscitation along the lines of Lazarus, but at the same time he can eat and can be touched, which forbids us to think in terms of a mirage. Both of these theories have been advanced as attempts to find alternatives to a belief in the resurrection, but neither of them can provide a satisfactory account of the evidence if it is taken as a whole.

Then there is the post-resurrection *teaching* of Jesus. For some reason we are not accustomed to looking at this in detail, but it is extremely important, because it was during this time that Jesus laid the foundation for the future teaching of the Church. In theological terms (if not necessarily in chronological order) pride of place belongs to the incident (recounted in Luke 24) of the meeting between Jesus and the two men on the road to Emmaus. On that occasion, Jesus pointed to the Old Testament and expounded the Christological hermeneutic which he had already talked about during his earthly ministry (John 5:39). He concluded his exposition with a repetition of the Last Supper, and it was at that point that he was recognised by the disciples – a paradigm of the relationship between Word and Sacrament which the Church was charged to maintain.

During his forty days on earth, Jesus also laid to rest speculation about the nature of the Kingdom which he was called to inherit. The disciples had been told any number of times that Jesus' Kingdom was not of this world, but after an event like the resurrection it is understandable that some of them might have felt that those earlier warnings no longer applied. But during the forty days, Jesus reinforced his earlier teaching on the subject and reminded them that the final consummation of all things remains a mystery concealed in the mind of the Father (Acts 1:7). Instead of promising an immediate parousia, he gave his disciples very specific commands, which lie at the heart of the Church's mission even now.

These commands are recorded for us in Matthew 28:19-20. They have frequently been regarded by scholars as inauthentic on the ground they contain a form of teaching, especially about the Trinity, which is too developed in sophistication to have been in existence at the beginning of the Church's life.

In response to this it can be pointed out that Jesus' basic command to preach and to baptise is one which he carried over from his earlier ministry. The difference is that after his death and resurrection, the content of the preaching was greatly increased, since in addition to the message of repentance there was now the promise of deliverance as well. This additional dimension to the Gospel message is reflected in our baptismal practice.

The use of the threefold name may appear to be unusually early if we are thinking primarily of the development of Trinitarian doctrine, but as we know that later Trinitarian doctrine grew out of baptismal practice and was not imposed on it, this should not surprise us unduly. The real question is where baptism in the threefold name may have come from, if it did not originate with Jesus himself. Who would have invented it, or thought of applying it to the sacrament? People who suggest that the Trinity is a complicated philosophical construction borrowed from various forms of Middle and Neo-Platonism have not reflected adequately on this phenomenon. Nor have they given sufficient consideration to some of the evidence which can be found in Acts, e.g. 8:15-17, where the point is made that baptism in the name of Christ *alone* is insufficient.

Taken as a whole, Jesus' post-resurrection teaching was a repetition and confirmation of his pre-resurrection message, not as a new departure brought about by the change in circumstances. This underlying continuity reinforces our belief that his death and resurrection were not accidental interruptions to a career which was intended to work out differently. On the contrary, they appear to have been the logical fulfilment of the whole dynamic of his teaching ministry. This is the standpoint of the Gospels, of course, even if some people would accuse them of a certain post-resurrection bias. The fact that the basic pattern of Christ's teaching and witness remained unaltered strongly supports the view that there is a deep-seated continuity between the 'before' and the 'after', which can only mean that the whole thing was planned that way from the beginning.

The final point which has to be made about the forty day period between Christ's resurrection and his ascension into Heaven is that it was unique to him. We shall share in his resurrection, but in our case, this will be combined with a kind of ascension into Heaven, which will occur simultaneously. We shall not spend a forty-day waiting period on earth, because there will be no point in our doing so. This in turn reminds us that our resurrection bodies will be somewhat different from his, in the sense that we shall experience the immediate transformation of our earthly nature into a heavenly one, whereas Christ's transformation took place in stages. His resurrection body, as it was during the forty days, was not earthly in the way that it had been before the crucifixion, but neither was it heavenly in the way that it is now. It was a body in transition from one dimension to the other, and it reflects certain characteristics of both. We are not going to go through this intermediate stage, because even those who are still alive on earth at his coming will rise to meet him in the air (1 Thess. 4:17). Paul even mentions that we shall be caught up in a cloud, which is the ultimate sign of the mysterious presence of God.

As Christians today it is vitally important that we rescue the resurrection from theological oblivion and restore it to the centre of our life and witness. Too often we have stopped with the *evidence* for its occurrence and neglected its deeper *meaning*. By doing this, we have missed out on a vital aspect of the gospel message, and have neglected the important transitional period from the life of Jesus to the life of the Church which bears witness to him. May God grant us wisdom to restore this aspect of his truth to its proper place so that we and the whole Church may recover something of the joy and wonder which the disciples must have felt on that first Easter morning.

9

The Ascension
(Acts 1:1-11)

The ascension of Jesus Christ into heaven forty days after his resurrection is probably the most inexplicable event in the Bible. People who want to deny the resurrection can always find a reason to doubt the Gospel accounts, however improbable their alternative explanation may be. Such people also find it easy to dismiss the virgin birth as a legend. The ascension, however, is another matter. It may just be plausible to say that the post-resurrection appearances of Jesus were hallucinations experienced by emotionally worked-up disciples. What cannot be explained is why this period should suddenly have come to an end, and in such a dramatic way. If the appearances were hallucinations, they would probably have become incredibly frequent for a time and then ceased when the frequency made them look implausible. On the other hand, if the disciples were genuinely convinced of their reality and were trying to explain it, it is far more likely that they would have said that Jesus was still around somewhere, and that he might suddenly appear again to any of them as he did in the upper room (and as he did, after his ascension, to Saul of Tarsus).

Theologians who concentrate on the 'Easter event' and

emphasize that in the post-Easter consciousness of the Church, the Jesus whom the disciples had known on earth was now the exalted Christ, often find the ascension an inconvenient detail and tend to ignore it. For them Christ was exalted in his resurrection, even though the Bible never says this. In Scripture there are two moments of exaltation – the crucifixion and the ascension, but not the resurrection! The Bible stubbornly insists that there was an intermediate period between the resurrection and the heavenly exaltation of Christ which forbids us from speaking of Easter as if it were the final act in the drama of man's redemption.

Recognition of such an intermediate period carries with it difficulties of its own however, which conservative Christians have been slow to face. For example, why was it that the resurrection body of Christ was not the final form which that body was to take? Why did it still need the exaltation of the ascension? Then too, what happened to the body when it ascended? Did it dissolve into spirit, or is it still present somewhere in heaven, or perhaps even in outer space? This sounds ridiculous to us, but when Yuri Gagarin went up into space in 1957, he is supposed to have reported that he did not find Christ there! From a rather different point of view, would it not have been better for us if Jesus had stayed on earth in his resurrected state, and gone about as a living witness to his saving work on the cross? Think how dramatic it would be if an evangelist could conjure up the risen Christ as the ultimate visual aid in his presentation of the gospel message! It is true that questions like these are not often asked, and to theologians they may appear to be naive or frivolous. But it would not be unfair to say that such questions have been ignored largely because the ascension itself is seldom discussed by anybody. But once we look at it closely, the problems come back to hit us in the face, and we find ourselves forced to look for satisfactory answers to questions which we might otherwise never have thought of asking.

When we turn to the Scriptures, we find that there is remarkably little evidence for us to go on, at least at first sight. The Gospels say virtually nothing about the ascension, even though they include something of the post-resurrection appearances and teaching of Jesus. Only John goes further, and then it is not in the narrative of the final chapter, but in the discourses of chapters 14–16 where we get some inkling of what is to happen. In these chapters, Jesus tells the disciples that he must go back to the Father, since only then will the Holy Spirit be able to come. But Jesus does not specify the manner of his departure, and we could not guess at an ascension merely from what John tells us.

The ascension is recorded in a single verse in Acts, and Luke leaves the impression, as do the other evangelists, that it is the second coming of Christ 'in the same manner' which is his chief concern. Paul is the only apostle who seems to have taken the ascension seriously, as an event of theological significance in its own right, but even he links it closely to Pentecost (Eph. 4:8-10). The Book of Revelation, of course, is written on the assumption that the ascension has already taken place, and its setting would be inconceivable without it, but in spite of all that, it cannot be said that John dwells on the subject as an event of significance in itself.

What are we to make of the apparent reluctance of Scripture to say much about the ascension of Christ? Does this silence mean that it does not have a central place in its teaching? Clearly the event was closely linked with what went before and after, but are we right to assume from this that the ascension is without any real importance of its own? Here we must be very careful. The early Church thought that the ascension was important enough to include it in the creeds – 'he ascended into heaven' – and the fact that it is not mentioned very frequently does not mean that it is of little importance. The same could equally well be said of other things, like the fall of Adam, yet the whole subsequent history of redemption depends on this single event! The ascension may be intimately bound up with its immediate context, but that does not mean that it cannot be regarded as having a significance all its own. In fact, as we shall see, it has an importance which goes far beyond what is apparent on the surface, and it is an event which has every right to claim our theological attention.

The ascension of Christ is presented in Scripture as the culmination of Jesus' post-resurrection witness. As we have already noticed, the forty-day period which this embraced is of great symbolic importance. Jesus spent forty days at the beginning of his ministry battling the temptations of Satan, and it is not surprising to find that he spent a similar period at the end of this earthly life consolidating his victory. It was during this period that the main lines of Jesus' pre-resurrection teaching became clear to the disciples. We cannot accept that they entered into a mature faith only in the wake of Pentecost, however important that event may have been. The sending of the Spirit brought power and conviction to the disciples, but not a new or deeper message. That had been given to them by Jesus before his ascension, as had the missionary command to evangelise and baptise the nations (Matt. 28:19-20). There is thus a very real sense in which the ascension represents the culmination of Jesus' earthly teaching and the completion of his message.

At the same time, we must be careful not to misconstrue this. The ascension may have signalled the completion of Jesus' message, but it certainly did not mean the end of his work. On the contrary, it marked the beginning of an entirely new phase in his work, one which affects us most directly today. It is true, of course, that Christ's great work of atonement was made and completed on the cross. It is also true that his resurrection meant that death had been defeated and eternal life given to those who believe. But in themselves these events were not the end of the story. The work which Christ accomplished on earth was on our behalf, but it was of no practical benefit to us until he ascended into Heaven. We should not forget that the only time that Jesus drew attention to his wounds was to rebuke the unbelief of Thomas. There was no mention of them as badges of his triumph over sin, though of course they were that as well. Their theological significance, however, was not fully revealed until after the ascension, when they became a mark of his present mission, which is to plead on our behalf at the right hand of the Father.

Christ's triumph over sin and his present work of intercession can only be understood in the context of this relationship to the Father, who had sent the Son into the world to make that work possible when he eventually returned to Heaven. It was only when the Son returned to the Father and presented his victory over sin and death to him for acceptance and confirmation, that it can be said that his task was truly over. Paul tells us this when he quotes Psalm 68 as an explanation of what happened in the ascension. When Jesus went up into heaven, he 'led captivity captive', or 'led a host of captives', which implies that this had not been done before. Perhaps we can express the matter best by saying that on the cross the captives had been *taken*, because it was then that sin had been paid for and death had been destroyed, but they were not *led away* until Christ ascended into Heaven.

This extra dimension is not simply a detail which we can afford to ignore. The Church's failure to reckon with it has meant that many Christians who have heard of the forgiveness of sins have no idea of this vital truth. God does not merely forgive our sins; he takes them away, as far as the east is from the west. This does not mean that we have become perfect; we still do things which are wrong, and still have to look to Christ for forgiveness and restoration. But what it does mean is that once we have been forgiven, we have no further reason to dwell on our sins, and they have no more power over us.

There are some people who are convinced that they have done such terrible things in their lives that they can never be forgiven. To them, the gospel message seems impossible, because they are totally overwhelmed by the wrongness of what they have done. These people have allowed something which is true – namely, that they are unworthy (as we all are) to receive the gift of God's grace – to become such a controlling principle in their lives that no forgiveness will ever be possible. Such people need to be reminded that when Christ ascended into heaven, he took their sins away with him, and there they remain – covered by his blood and buried in his love. If, once we are Christians, we go looking for our sins, if we are tempted to dig them up and dwell on them in a spirit of morbid fascination, then we will find nothing and no one but Christ. Our sins are hidden with him in God, and they will never again emerge to trouble us.

In an age when few people appear to take sin seriously, and where guilt can be explained away by psychology, it may seem surprising that there should be so many people in this position. But this is a spiritual difficulty which afflicts believers, not those who are outside the Church and who know nothing of the grace of God. The nature of sin is such that we do not really begin to understand it until we are set free from it, and can see it for what it truly is. People who live in the dark have no idea what they are missing, but when the light shines on them, their eyes get sore and take time to adjust. Usually this works reasonably well, but there are cases where people develop a morbid fear of the darkness they have left behind and are convinced that it is waiting in the wings to claim them back. They cannot go forward as they should because they are trapped – paralysed in a sense – by the peculiar kind of fear which comes from knowledge. You or I might be able to walk down the high street without thinking about where we are going, but picture the ex-convict, or drug addict, who sees the same street differently. He knows where the crooks hide, where the drugs can be obtained, who is into what. He may have been set free from all that now, but the knowledge remains to haunt him, and he is afraid to go where the rest of us walk without thinking twice about it.

There is a sense in which all Christians are ex-convicts. We are sinners who have been saved by grace, but the awareness of those sins remains in our minds, and can prey on our fears of falling back into them. This is why it is so important to be told again and again that those sins are locked away and can never get out again, because Christ has taken them off the earth, and lost them in the boundless depths of Heaven. Christ does not hold out his wounds to *us*, as a reminder of the evil we have done; rather, he presents them to the *Father*, as a plea for mercy on our behalf. When Jesus took his atoning sacrifice into heaven, he did so in order to become our mediator, using it as the basis on which to plead for our deliverance from eternal punishment and death. His work on the cross cannot be limited to its historical dimension alone, important though that is. Protestants have been so concerned to affirm the 'once for all' character of Christ's saving work that we have sometimes forgotten, or at least underemphasized, its ongoing significance.

The atonement is a work of Christ which continues to function on our behalf in the heavenly places. His blood, shed 'once for all' at Calvary, remains the only sacrifice for our sins, but that sacrifice has been presented to God the Father in eternity. Far from undercutting traditional Protestant teaching, this understanding actually goes a long way to refute any notion of the mass being a sacrifice. To be fair to them, modern Catholics insist that there can be no repetition of Christ's work on earth, and claim that when Protestants accuse them of trying to repeat the sacrifice of Calvary in the celebration of the eucharist, they are guilty of a serious misunderstanding. Perhaps it is a misunderstanding which has been shared by millions of uneducated Catholic believers, but it is still a mistake nonetheless. But Catholics like to think of the mass as something which enables us to 'enter into the movement of Christ's self-offering' as one recent Anglican-Roman Catholic dialogue put it.

The idea is that Christ's historical offering must be made 'real' for us, and this can only happen if it is also in some way present in our experience. From this comes the great importance attached to the notion of Christ's 'real presence' in the eucharist, a doctrine which it may be hard (or impossible) to tie down in physical terms, but which is essential all the same. Christ's sacrifice must be here, with us now, in the broken bread and in the poured-out wine. We may have problems with a term like 'transubstantiation', which really only makes sense against a background of Aristotelian physics, which everyone has now abandoned, but what those medieval theologians were trying to express remains valid.

Protestants agree with Catholics about the importance of making Christ's sacrifice 'real' in our present experience, and in this respect we can accept that their intentions, at least, are certainly right. However, we disagree with them about the way in which this process of making Christ's sacrifice 'real' actually occurs. To our way of thinking, it is not the heavenly sacrifice which comes down to earth in a kind of reincarnation (which is what transubstantiation amounts to). Rather, it is the earthly church which is called to rise with Christ to the heavenly places, where we are seated with him in glory (Eph. 2:6).

This was not a doctrine discovered by Luther or Calvin in the sixteenth century. It was the achievement of Augustine (354-430) to have made it clear that in the ascension the body of Christ returned to the Father, and that if we are to gain access to it we must rise in the power of the Holy Spirit to be with him. The 'real presence' is not in bread or wine, but in the heart of every believer, who knows that by the shed blood of Christ, taken into Heaven at his ascension, we have access to the Father.

At a personal level, the ascension is a guarantee that our manhood has been redeemed – 'taken up into God', in the words of the Athanasian Creed. In this connection, Christians are apt to fall into one of two contrary errors. Either they reject life on earth, preferring only to wait for the end, or they try to achieve perfection here and now in a kind of social utopia. It is in the light of the glorious ascension that these tendencies are checked and put in perspective. The value of earthly things is most truly seen in the perspective of the biblical hope of eternal fulfilment. We who follow after Christ are looking for the place which he has gone to prepare for us (John 14:2). Our eyes have been opened to the heavenly realities and, because that has happened, the purpose of our life on earth is made clear. The ascension of Christ is the bond between time and eternity, the guarantee that we have been saved, and the means by which we now enjoy fellowship with him – in and for eternity.

10

The Heavenly Session of Christ
(Hebrews 10:12-18)

The 'heavenly session' is a rather odd-sounding name given to what is perhaps the most immediately important part of Christ's entire life and work. Today the word 'session' normally means the meeting of a committee or a legislative body, and we are likely to get the wrong idea of what is going on in Heaven. Originally, the word simply meant 'seating', and it is this sense which is preserved here. The heavenly session of Christ is what is described in the Apostles' Creed, where it says of Christ that 'he ascended into Heaven, and sits at the right hand of the Father'.

Another possible misunderstanding comes from the way we normally think of sitting down today. To us, the words convey a sense of rest. If we have been working hard, or are not feeling well, we want to sit down for a while, and take the load off our feet. After going through the crucifixion, the resurrection and the ascension, who could blame Jesus if he felt the same way? Probably that is what most people subconsciously imagine when they hear the words of the Creed, because it seems like the natural thing to do at that point.

In fact, of course, the heavenly session is not a rest at

all, but the beginning of an entirely new work of God. We have already seen something of this in our discussion of the ascension, and we must now look at it more fully. When Christ sat down, he sat down at 'the right hand of God'. This is a symbolic way of saying that he assumed the power of God, because the right hand was the one in which the king held the sceptre, and whoever sat on the king's right was the most powerful and trusted minister in the kingdom. This is the place which now belongs to Christ, and is a reminder to us of what his triumph over sin and death really means.

Jesus told his disciples that he had to go back to his Father, and that this would be better for them, because on his return a whole new spiritual power would be released, and they would do far greater things than he had done in their midst (John 16). At first sight this sounds strange, and the disciples were duly puzzled by Jesus' words. How would it be possible for them to do greater things than the miracles which they had witnessed with their own eyes, but which they knew perfectly well they could never hope to do themselves? On a theological level, if Jesus was really who he said he was, how could there be another person, the mysterious 'Comforter', who would do even greater things? How could anyone be greater than the Son of God?

These things confused the disciples because at the time Jesus told them what was going to happen, it was all still in the future. They did not understand that in returning to the Father, he was going to assume the Father's power, and continue to work in and through them by means of the Comforter who was to come. In other words, his departure would not be an abandonment of the disciples to their own devices, but would lead to an enhanced relationship with them, which in turn would empower the disciples and release them for a ministry of which they could not as yet dream.

The heavenly session is therefore primarily about Christ's kingly rule, through the Comforter whom he has sent, in the lives of his followers on earth. This is why it is the aspect of his life and work which is most immediately relevant to us, because it affects what we do and how we live right now. Without the heavenly session of Christ, the Comforter would not have come, and there would be no Christian experience, and no Christian Church today – it is as simple and as all-embracing as that. It is because Christ is seated at the right hand of God the Father that we can be the people we are, and can do the things which he has commanded us to do, with the assurance that our work for him will not be wasted.

The first point to remember about the heavenly session of Christ is that it is the sign that all the forces of evil, which are opposed to him, have been defeated. It is true that we still experience evil in the world, and that we still have to struggle against Satan, but although there are battles ahead, the war itself has been decided. We can perhaps understand this by drawing a parallel with the Second World War. It was reasonably clear after the great battles of Stalingrad and El Alamein that Hitler was defeated and that he had no hope of winning in the end. As time went on, that fact became even clearer.

A wise man, knowing that he could never win, would have sued for peace and tried to get the best terms possible. But Hitler did not do that, and with very few exceptions, an entire nation followed him along the road to ruin. Why did they do this? Because the power which held them in thrall was an evil spiritual force, which was capable of blinding its subjects and forcing them to do what they would never have contemplated in their right mind. Only the destruction of the ultimate source of that power could set them free from it, and when that happened the scales fell from their eyes. People often remark how surprising it was that postwar Germany had so few Nazis, and many thought that this was simply hypocrisy – that underneath the surface, most Germans continued to support Hitler's ideas as they had before. But of course this was not true. It was as if the entire nation had been hypnotised and deluded, and when it woke up, the whole thing appeared to be a bad dream which they could hardly believe they had ever participated in.

This is a good picture of the nature of Satan's rule today. The cross and the resurrection are the great battles which have decided the war, and the followers of Christ, even if they continue to live on enemy-occupied territory, know that they have won. If Satan were sensible, he would surrender, and perhaps even ask God's forgiveness for the wrong he has done. But of course the minute we say this we realise how impossible it is. Satan is in the grip of his own pride, and he has the power to mesmerise others into obeying him. Most of his subjects have no idea at all what they are doing; as far as they are concerned, evil is just part of everyday reality. It is only when the spell is broken, and they wake up to new life in Christ, that the whole thing appears absurd and incomprehensible. We know this perfectly well, because it has happened to us. Before we became Christians we had no idea that we were living in sin, and if anyone told us so, we probably mocked them or simply turned away in total incomprehension. But once the light dawned, we understood, and now we are part of Christ's great army, waiting for the day when his enemies will finally be smashed under his feet (Heb. 10:13).

The second point about Christ's heavenly session is that we now have a new focus for our allegiance. We are not followers of an earthly prophet, as the disciples to some extent were, but servants of a heavenly King. This means that Heaven is now our homeland, even though we have never been there. This may seem strange, but every once in a while we meet people who are genuine expatriates. They may have been born in India or Argentina, and lived all their lives in some remote corner of the globe, but when we meet them, we think that they are more British than the British. And of course, in some ways, they are, because their background and environment have forced them to make a choice. Either they could assimilate to the country where they were born, or they could seek to preserve their distinctiveness. Those who chose the second option had to work at it, so that no-one would be able to distinguish them from the original. This is what Christians are called to be like. We are not holy by nature, as the angels in heaven are holy, and everything around us conspires to take us away from that ideal. But as expatriate citizens of the kingdom of Heaven we have to persevere, and we are aided and strengthened in our resolve by the presence of the Holy Spirit, the Comforter whom Jesus promised to send to his disciples.

This is the third and perhaps most important aspect of the heavenly session of Christ. When he sat down at the right hand of God, he gave gifts to men, said the Apostle Paul (Eph. 4:8), quoting Psalm 68:18 in order to make his point. These gifts are dispensed to us by the Comforter, the Holy Spirit whom Jesus has sent, in order to make his kingdom on earth a living and present reality. A Christian is a person in whom the Holy Spirit dwells, and who has therefore received a share of his gifts. The rise of the charismatic movement in the past generation has brought this very much to the fore once more, and there are few if any churchgoers today who have never heard of the 'spiritual gifts'. Unfortunately though, this term has come to be used of a specific type of gift, which is characterised by a certain dramatic and esoteric quality. Speaking in tongues is the classic example, but it is by no means always the most prominent of the gifts which are talked about. Very often one will hear about the gift of healing, of 'knowledge', of power of different kinds.

These gifts are often mentioned in Scripture, but not always. The 'falling down phenomenon', for example, which was associated with the so-called Toronto blessing, cannot be found anywhere in the Bible, nor can most of the other manifestations (like uncontrollable laughter) which are associated with it. Much the same can be said for other occurrences of 'spiritual outpouring' which have been reported in different places. A few Christian leaders have denounced this kind of thing, but most have just let it pass, believing that it will soon fade away and that little lasting harm is done. In one sense that is no doubt true, and the said phenomena probably do not deserve a full-scale refutation because they will die out once the novelty has worn off.

The real problem with these things is not that they will leave generations of scarred and embittered ex-Christians, though perhaps there are a few such casualties along the road. More insidious is the danger that Christians in general will come to associate the words 'spiritual gifts' with such things, and therefore be turned away from the reality of which the Bible speaks. We are called to be people who are filled with the Holy Spirit – what a tragedy it would be if we came to think of that primarily as a form of behaviour which is abnormal, and even bordering on the insane. The apostle Paul warned the Corinthian church not to give the wrong impression, because others would be turned off the gospel. Today we need to heed that warning, and reconsider just exactly what it means to be 'filled with the Spirit'.

First of all, a Spirit-filled person is a person who is changed in heart, mind and behaviour. It is easy to say this kind of thing, but very difficult to translate it into practice. If Christ is King in our lives, then this will manifest itself in love, joy, peace, patience and all the fruits of the Spirit which Paul lists in Galatians 5:22. These things do not come naturally, and they cannot be sustained without the grace of God at work in us. Love, for example, is not merely an attraction to people and things we happen to like – true love is a sacrificial self-giving to and for others, whether we like them or not. Joy is not to be confused with enjoyment – it is a serene countenance which sees the true end of all things in Christ, whether they happen to be enjoyable or not. And so on. Furthermore, the fruits of the Spirit are not optional, nor are they divided out among different believers in the way that the gifts are. You do not have to speak in tongues in order to be a believer, but you do have to show something of God's love, as Paul did not hesitate to remind the Corinthians (1 Cor. 13).

More harm has been done to Christ's kingdom on earth by Christians who have ignored this truth than almost anything else. Today the Church is often weak and divided because there is no love in it, no joy, no peace, no patience, no humility. Sometimes it is even because people insist on exercising their particular gift without regard for these underlying principles, which has brought trouble to the Body of Christ. This can happen in individual congregations, and it can happen at the highest level as well. The Papacy, for example, likes to claim that its spiritual gift is to promote the unity of all Christians in the truth of the gospel, but the way in which it has exercised this gift (if indeed the claim is justified) has left a divided Christendom and continues to be one of the main barriers preventing the reunion of the churches!

It is in the context of the fruits that the gifts of the Spirit are meant to be manifested. These gifts are listed in the New Testament in what appears to be a kind of hierarchical order – with speaking in tongues placed very firmly at the bottom. A church which emphasises that sort of thing to the exclusion of the others is not spiritually advanced, but spiritually immature. Furthermore, speaking in tongues is mentioned only when it caused a problem, as it did in the Corinthian church. Elsewhere, as in Ephesians 4:11, it does not appear at all.

The greatest of the gifts is the apostleship, which was given to the disciples who saw the Risen Christ. This included the apostle Paul, who described himself as 'one born out of due time' (1 Cor. 15:8), because he had not been one of the original disciples and had even persecuted the Church before his conversion. The apostleship is important because it is a teaching office, given to these men so that they could record, either by themselves or through people authorised by them, the true message of Jesus. This had three parts – the past (the earthly ministry of Jesus, recorded for us in the Gospels), the present (the life and troubles of the existing churches, recorded for us in the Acts and in the Epistles) and the future (Christ's final victory and the end of all things, recorded for us in the book of Revelation). This witness, which is collectively known as the New Testament, is the constitution of the Christian Church, telling us how Christ's kingly rule is to be worked out in human history.

Prophecy is another spiritual gift which is given to the Church, though it is not altogether clear what is meant by this. Some people think that the prophets of the New Testament are really the same as the apostles, because they delivered the inspired Word of God. Others think that 'prophets' refers mainly to preachers of the Word, who were inspired to apply the teaching of the apostles to the lives of believers, but did not receive new revelation themselves. Still others think of 'prophets' primarily in Old Testament terms, and regard them as Christians who receive additional revelation from God, even today. Of these possibilities, it is the second which appears to be most in accord with what Paul meant in Ephesians 4:11. There would have been little point in repeating the apostolic gift in a list of only four or five things, and the apostolic gift left no room for further revelation in the Old Testament sense. What we have here are preachers who are called to exhort people to hear and obey the Word of God.

Third in the list are the evangelists, those who are called to spread the gospel. Obviously this is a work which concerned the apostles and the prophets as well, but evangelists have a special focus to their ministry, which is winning unbelievers for Christ. Many Christians believe that this is the work of the minister, but this is not necessarily so. Some ministers are gifted evangelists, but not all are, nor is it necessary for them to be. Conversely, not all evangelists are called to be clergy. The missionary task must be pursued in many different ways and it embraces a wide range of people. A translator of books for distribution in another country is as much an evangelist as a Christian professor in a secular university, who stands up for his faith and defends it against rationalistic and other forms of attack. But preaching the gospel remains the primary aim of every evangelist, since it is by preaching that faith is born (Rom. 10:14-17).

Next, and last in this list, are the pastors and teachers. Again, many people associate these things with the ordained minister and, as with the above, there is a clear overlap here. Ordained people do have to act as pastors, and they do have to teach as well, but these tasks are subsidiary to the calling to preach. In fact, many ordinary church members act as pastors and as teachers, either in the home, or in small groups, or in institutions like the Sunday school. In the Body of Christ we minister to one another most often at this level. Nor is this to be despised, because without proper nurture and good teaching, how can we become evangelists or preachers? These things may seem like lesser gifts because they are more widespread and less prominent, but they are foundational for everything else.

We have now seen how Christ governs the kingdom which God the Father has given to him. Seated on his heavenly throne, he is in full control of all that is going on, and nothing is too small to escape his attention. Far from being a distant king, he has given us his Holy Spirit, not only so that we may apply his teaching on earth, but also so that we may communicate with him in Heaven. Prayer is the means by which we open ourselves up to God and discover his will for us on a day-to-day basis. We can measure our closeness to God and the strength of our relationship with Christ by the quality of our prayer life – a frightening, but realistic measurement. Christ is not ruling in our hearts if we are not in constant touch with him, nor are we pointing in the right direction for our lives, and for the advancement of his kingdom. May God the Father grant us the vision of his Son reigning in glory and send us to our knees, in the power of his Holy Spirit, that we might be true and faithful servants of his heavenly kingdom.

11

The Second Coming of Christ
(1 Thessalonians 4:13-5:11)

The heavenly session of Christ marks the fulfilment of his saving work, but it is not the end of the story. The Bible tells us in many places that he will come again in order to take us up to be with him and to put an end to sin, suffering and death. There is no doubt that this hope was very real in the early Church, and that it sustained men like the apostle Paul as they faced the dangers which nature and a hostile world placed in the way of the growing Church. Modern scholars have sometimes interpreted this to mean that the first Christians believed that most of them would live to see Christ's second coming, and that this belief affected the way in which they went about their evangelistic activity. In the early days, so it is said, little attention was paid to matters of Church organisation, doctrine and the like, because the priority was to get as many believers into the kingdom as possible. Only as time went on and the first generation died out did it become apparent that the hope of Christ's return was not going to materialise. When this eventually sank it, the Church changed its character. Having been a fairly loose organisation, it now became structured and disciplined, with a clear sense of hierarchy and a system of discipline which rigorously excluded dissidents, who were branded as heretics.

It is hardly necessary to say that such a picture is oversimplified, and would be a caricature even if elements of it were true. But even a cursory reading of the New Testament shows that the reality was very different from the picture painted above. First of all, there was always a structure of authority in the Church. That authority came primarily from Christ, and was delegated to the apostles in the first instance and to men appointed by them in the second. We can trace this development very clearly. When Saul of Tarsus was converted, in the very early days, he could not just go out and start preaching the gospel with or without the blessing of other Christians. He was obliged to seek the approval of Peter and the council of the apostles at Jerusalem, and although he later disagreed with them, he was never out of fellowship with the mother church. Later on, Paul also appointed men like Timothy and Titus to carry on his work, and they in turn found others to run the churches at the local level.

Secondly, the Church always had a clear notion of right and wrong in matters of doctrine, even if there were a number of blurs around the edges. For example, there were some evangelists who were baptising Samaritans in the name of Jesus only, forgetting that the Lord had commanded them to baptise in the name of the Father, the Son and the Holy Spirit. When the apostles at Jerusalem heard this, and realised that the new converts had not received the Spirit, they went down to Samaria themselves and laid hands on them (Acts 8:14-17). Had they been unclear about this, or had there been no structure of command and authority, it is hard to imagine such an incident ever taking place. At the same time, there were people who wanted to take advantage of what they saw as a new spiritual power in the world, and were even prepared to buy it. Such was the case of Simon Magus (Acts 8:18-19), who was told quite firmly that he had no licence to preach the gospel. False teachers abounded in the first generation, and it is largely to counteract them that much of the New Testament was written, but there is never any suggestion that the apostles welcomed theological diversity or pluralism in the modern sense.

Their expectation of the second coming of Christ must therefore be seen in this light. They were well aware that not all the promises of God had as yet been fulfilled in Christ, and they accepted the angels' promise, made at his ascension into Heaven, that he would return in the same way at some unspecified future time (Acts 1:11). But there is no evidence to suggest that this hope diminished as a result of disappointment at the delay, or that the Church changed its character as a result.

The future is always an unknown quantity, and this is reflected in language as much as in anything else. Students of Latin and Greek learn that hypothetical or untrue statements are liable to be put in the subjunctive mood, to indicate that they are not real. We do this sometimes in English ('If I were ill, I would not be here now.'), but are less consistent. But in Latin at least, there is no future subjunctive, because the hard-headed Romans knew that all future statements are by definition hypothetical, so they did not need a special mood to express this. In our modern world we have become so future-oriented that we are in serious danger of losing sight of this fundamental fact. We plan years in advance, take out long-term mortgage and insurance policies, speculate on what the world will be like in a hundred years' time and so on. Predicting the future is no longer the gift of prophets, but the common coin of social analysts everywhere.

Of course, we do not have to look very far to see how foolish this is. All we have to do is go back to Jules Verne, for example, and read what he thought the future would hold. Some of it has happened, much of it has not, and a good deal seems as fantastic to us as it did to those who first read about it in the late nineteenth century. On the other hand, there have been inventions, like computers, which Verne did not know about, but which have changed our lives more profoundly than most other things he mentions, and in a very short time as well. Or look at George Orwell's famous *1984*, which predicted a world governed by thought police and reduced to a slavery worse than that of ancient Egypt. Is that how you remember 1984?

A sense of the basic unpredictability of the future is something which we need to recover a sense of if we are ever going to understand the New Testament hope in the second coming of Christ. Someone like the apostle Paul would have thought it pointless, and perhaps even quite mad, to sit down and predict what would happen in the year 200, for example, and he certainly did not plan the Church with that in mind. He lived in and for the present, as indeed Jesus had taught his disciples to do (Matt. 6:34). At the same time, he was not so engrossed in what he was doing that he had no sense of purpose, and no vision of where it was all headed. Paul evangelised because he knew that this was all part of Christ's preparation for his second coming, and on occasion he actually told his converts as much. They worried about what would happen to them when they died, and when Christ would come again, but he put their minds to rest.

He did not do this by setting out a detailed timetable of events, but by reminding his hearers of the general principles which governed the belief in a second coming. First, he pointed out that Jesus' return was part of a complete plan of salvation, most of which was already accomplished. If you have problems trusting in God for the future, said Paul, then look at what he has already done in the past. The Christians he was writing to could easily point to the life, death and resurrection of Jesus as evidence of God's work among them in the recent past, and to that they could add their own experience. We are further removed from the historical events, but conversely we have a great deal more experience that we can point to. Who in Paul's day could have imagined a worldwide Church with millions of believers, a deep spiritual and theological tradition and a whole civilisation to its credit? Could a tiny huddle of frightened worshippers in the catacombs of Rome have ever imagined that one day their city would be full of churches and cathedrals, all dedicated to the name of Christ? Christ's work continues to grow and expand, and we who follow after can point to it as assurance that he has not abandoned his people.

This, indeed, is Paul's second point. Christ in Heaven is still very much in charge, as the work of the Church demonstrates. When he returns, it will not be as a kind of Robinson Crusoe, coming back after being lost at the ends of the earth. Nor will he be a Rip van Winkle, waking up after several centuries to a world which has passed him by. On the contrary, Christ will return to a world which he has never really left, at least not in spirit. His final reign will be an extension and completion of what is already happening, not some new and surprising development which no-one, including he, had really expected.

When Christ comes again, his arrival will be heralded by an archangel blowing God's trumpet – the symbol of final victory which would have been familiar to his hearers. It will come as a complete surprise to those who are not prepared for it, but those of us who are already living in the light of Christ will not be caught off guard. This is a reminder to us that the second coming of Christ is the culmination of our spiritual warfare, the final defeat of Satan and the last judgement. Judgement is not a popular idea, and it is not surprising that little is said about it nowadays. Sometimes this neglect is justified by pointing to what were supposed to have been distortions of the idea in the past. A favourite target is Jonathan Edwards' *Sinners in the hand of an angry God*, which is a classic work of the mid-eighteenth-century revival. The impression is vaguely given that such a title is psychologically unbalanced, and that the converts who resulted from it were frightened into the kingdom of God by fears of hellfire and brimstone.

Anyone who might be inclined to think like that need only look to the hymns which the revival produced to see that this is a gross distortion of the facts. Charles Wesley's *O for a thousand tongues to sing* or John Newton's *Amazing grace*, to name but two, are hardly monuments to spiritual depression. And would Welsh rugby fans belt out *Arglwydd arwain trwy'r anialwch* (*Guide me, O thou great Jehovah*) if they thought they were going to lose? Yet William Williams, who composed it and later translated it into English, was a product of the 'angry God' school of thought if ever there was one.

Judgement will come to us all when Christ returns (1 Cor. 3:11-15), but it is a terror only to those who are afraid of what might happen to them. Here we have hit upon the real root of the reluctance to say much about it these days. People who lack assurance of their own salvation are going to be very wary of contemplating the alternative, because at the back of their minds there will always be the feeling that this might be applicable to them. Obviously, we do not want to go to the other extreme and rejoice at the thought of our enemies roasting in hell, but that is not the true alternative. When we contemplate judgement at the hand of God, we have no reason for complacency. In a sense, we shall all be condemned, because we have all sinned and fallen short of his glory (Rom. 3:23). There is certainly nothing to boast about there.

What makes Christians different is not that we have

sinned less than others, or that we have some special claim on God's mercy because of what we have managed to achieve on his behalf. Not at all. What makes us different is that Christ has chosen us to belong to him, that he has paid the price for our sins so that it might be possible for us to dwell in his presence, and that he has actually called us out from the world around us to be his servants and witnesses. We are not judged by him, only because he has taken our judgement on himself. At the last judgement it is that which we shall see – the price which has been paid on our behalf. Far from spending our time rejoicing in the fate of the wicked, we shall be overwhelmed with humility and gratitude, as we see for the first time with our own eyes the Lamb who was slain before the foundation of the world (Rev. 13:8).

Knowing this, we should not be reticent to preach the judgement which will come, because it is the terrible reality which the world will have to face. We do not want anyone to be able to turn to us and cry out: 'But you never told me!' when that great and terrible day of the Lord finally comes. Yet how many of us hold back from preaching the judgement of God, precisely because we are not fully convinced that we have either the right or the obligation to do so?

When Christ comes again, there will be a general resurrection of the dead, which will take place immediately before the judgement. For many centuries, Christians preferred to bury their dead rather than have them cremated because they thought in crudely simplistic terms. You can't rise from the dead, they reasoned, if there is nothing left of you to rise! Of course this was naive, and we must not imagine that the New Testament church thought in that way, because cremation was a standard form of burial in the ancient world. To those who want to know what we shall look like when we come back again, Paul gave the perfect answer (1 Cor. 15:35-49). The bodies we have now are like seeds which have to be planted and die if the fruit is ever to grow. We cannot tell from looking at the seeds what the plants which come from them will look like – there is really no comparison at all between them. I may want to come back looking like Mr (or Miss) Universe, but what I shall be in the resurrection is infinitely more glorious than that, so glorious in fact that I simply cannot imagine it now. Speculation about that sort of thing is foolish, Paul tells us, because we are talking about a different kind of reality altogether. 'Flesh and blood cannot inherit the kingdom of God' (1 Cor. 15:50).

Those who are still alive when Christ comes again will 'rise to meet him in the air' (1 Thess. 4:17) where we shall be reunited with those who have already died. This is a curious detail, but it is best to understand it in the light of Christ's ascension. At that time, he rose into the air and was taken up by the clouds of Heaven, which is the exact parallel of what will happen to us. In other words, where there was a real time distinction between Christ's resurrection and his ascension, in our case the two events will be more or less simultaneous, perhaps with a pause for the last judgement, though it is probable that that too will be automatic when it actually happens.

To be caught up in the cloud is to be caught up in God, because the cloud is the symbol of the divine presence.

The transformation which we shall undergo at Christ's second coming is but a part of a wider change which will overtake the entire creation. In his great vision of the end of time, John saw 'a new heaven and a new earth' (Rev. 21:1). The creation as we know it, with all its sins, its sorrows and its inadequacies, will be entirely swept away. In its place will be the New Jerusalem, which will come down from heaven and form the centrepiece of this new reality.

Obviously, the last two chapters of the book of Revelation, like most of the rest of it, are highly symbolic, and we must be careful not to interpret them too literally. But even within the context of the symbolism there is much that we can learn. First of all, the new creation will be a city, not a garden, as the first creation was. In other words, it will embrace man's creative ability, and even some aspect of his rebellion against God, because the first cities were built by men who wanted to challenge God's rule of the universe (Gen. 11:4).

The heavenly city will be Jerusalem, the capital of the covenant which God made with his people Israel. The whole of sacred history will be reunited in it, but one element will be missing. In the earthly Jerusalem there was a temple, which formed the religious heart of the city. But in the New Jerusalem there will be no temple, because the presence of God will take its place (Rev. 21:22). In that city, the Lamb will sit on his throne, reigning with his saints in eternal light, and embarking on a life far more wonderful than anything which we have ever known, or can ever know, here on earth. The message of the second coming of Christ is that the best is yet to come. What we have to look forward to is life, and glory everlasting. Jesus concludes his great revelation to John with the assurance that he is coming quickly. What more can we do than respond with the apostle, and say: 'Amen. Come, Lord Jesus.'

Scripture Index

Genesis
11:4 123
22 41
Deuteronomy
6:13 57
6:16 55
8:3 52
Psalms
68 96
68:18 107
69:21 77
91:11-12 54
Isaiah
7:14 19
53:3 78
Jeremiah
1:6 24
Daniel
8:16 20
9:21 20
Malachi
4:5 40
Matthew
1:18-19 19
1:18 19
2:3 21
3:13-17 36
3:15 43
4:1-11 47
5:11 78
6:34 118
10:34 78
12:48-50 76
16:16 82
16:17 31
16:24 79
17:1-9 59
27:32-56 69
28 81
28:19 43
28:19-20 88, 95

Mark
1:9-13 36
9:2-10 59
10:29 76
15:21-41 69
16 81
Luke
1:19 20
1:26-38 16
1:28 22
1:29 23
1:31 21
1:32 25
1:43 18
1:56 18
3:21-22 36
9:28-36 59
9:34 66
23:26-29 69
24 81
24:13-35 84
John
1:1 5
1:11 78
1:14 27, 30, 31, 33
1:29 38
1:29-34 36
4:22 43
5:18 8
5:39 34, 87
14–16 93
14:2 101
15:14 57
16 103
19:16-37 69
19:26-27 75
19:28 77
20-21 81

Acts
1:1-11 91
1:6 41
1:6-7 82
1:7 87
1:11 116
1:21-22 32
8:14-17 115
8:15-17 88
8:18-19 116
Romans
3:23 120
8:3 30
8:18 80
8:18-19 66
10:14-17 112
1 Corinthians
2:2 70
3:11-15 120
10:4 13
10:13 50
11:1 38
13 109
13:12 67
15:8 110
15:17 81
15:35-49 122
15:50 122
2 Corinthians
4:10 74, 85
Galatians
2:20 75
4:6 8
5:22 108
6:17 74
Ephesians
2:6 15,100
2:18 15
4:8 107
4:8-10 93
4:11 110, 111

Philippians
2:5-11 26
3:10 75
Colossians
1:16-17 10
1 Thessalonians
4-5 81
4:13-5:11 114
4:17 90,122
2 Timothy
2:12 74
Hebrews
4:15 50
10:12-18 102
10:13 106
1 Peter
4:13 75
2 Peter
1:16-18 63
1 John
4:16 12
Revelation
13:8 121
21:1 123
21: 22

Selected themes

Adoptionism 37-8, 42
Antinomianism 19, 20
Arius 11
Atonement 69-74, 81-84, 95, 98, 99
Christ
    Annunciation of, 16-25
    Ascension of, 89, 91-101, 102, 116, 122
    Baptism of, 36-46
    Crucifixion of, 69-80, 92, 102
    Divinity of, 6, 9, 30, 33, 42, 50, 53, 60, 61, 68, 73, 86
    Exaltation of, 92
    Fulfilment of Old Testament 7, 35, 36, 38, 40-42, 63, 87
    Heavenly session of, 102-113
    Humanity of, 6, 30, 31, 33, 42, 47-50, 61, 68, 71, 86
    Incarnation of, 6, 16, 25, 26-35, 62, 81
    Misunderstood by Jews 21, 41, 78
    Naming 21
    Pre-incarnation Appearances of Christ 13, 14
    Recognition of, 31
    Rejection of, 31, 78
    Renunciation of, 75, 76
    Resurrection of, 6, 79, 81-90, 91, 92, 95, 102, 105, 122, 124
    Second coming 93, 114-124
    Suffering of, 41, 74-79, 83, 85
    Teaching of, 8, 34, 42, 68, 76, 78, 85, 87-89, 95, 118
    Temptations of, 47-58, 94
    Transfiguration of, 59-68, 81
    Virgin birth of, 16, 19, 91
    The Word 5, 9-11, 27, 29-31, 33, 34

Christians in God's presence 15, 25, 58, 63, 69, 72-74, 81, 83, 90, 100, 101, 112, 121-124

Church as body of Christ 34, 62, 109, 112
Condemnation 6
Forgiveness of sins 36-38, 43, 69, 72, 83, 96-98
God's sovereignty 19, 123
Grace 22, 23, 37, 97, 98, 109
Greek Thought 29, 39, 88
Holiness of God 14
Hysteria / Hallucinations 86, 91
John the Baptist 17, 18, 36-40
Judgement 65, 71, 72, 119-122
Justification 74, 75
Kingdom of God 21, 37, 41, 46, 57, 85, 87, 112, 113
Love of God 12, 13, 109
Mariolatry 17, 22, 23, 62
Obedience 19, 20, 23, 24, 52, 57, 79, 80, 84
Redemption 6, 62, 65, 69, 73, 83, 92, 94, 100, 121
Resurrection 6, 79, 81-90, 91, 92, 95, 102, 105, 121, 122, 124
Revelation 6, 14, 15, 28, 29, 31, 33, 35, 42, 60, 66, 67, 123, 124
Sanctification 74, 75
Spiritual Gifts 107-112
Taborites 59
The Trinity 7, 8, 24, 25, 42, 73, 88, 115
    Father 8, 10-13, 15, 42, 43, 68, 72, 83, 87, 93, 96, 98, 99, 100, 103, 104, 112, 113
    Son 9-13, 15, 29, 30, 32, 35, 38, 42, 45, 50, 67, 96, 103, 113
    Holy Spirit 19, 34, 35, 42, 93, 95, 100, 103, 104, 107, 108, 112, 113, 115
Weakness of Flesh 50, 64, 65, 70

Gerald Bray is Anglican Professor of Divinity at Beeson Divinity School, Samford University, Birmingham, Alabama. Previously he taught Christian Doctrine at Oak Hill College, London. He also edits the Anglican scholarly journal, Churchman. Christian Focus also publishes his *Creeds, Councils and Christ* (ISBN 1 85792 280 8), a study of the early church.